RUIN.

collage art and mixed media art
by Jolie Ruin

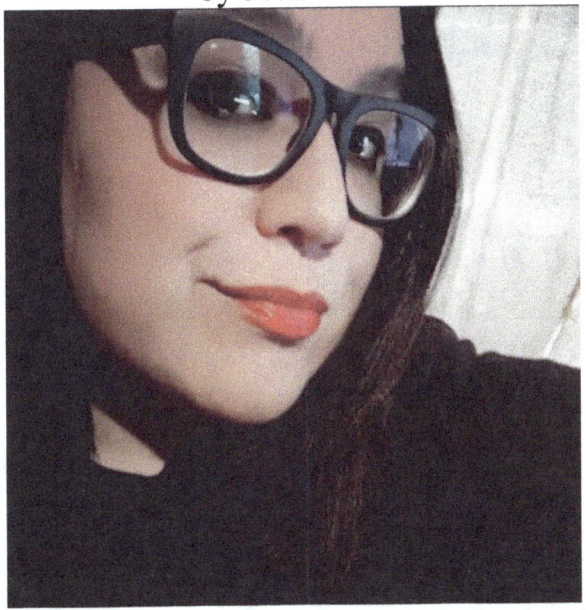

You can find me and my art on social media as
@JolieRuin and @RiotGrrrlPress

And you can purchase my art, zines, t-shirts and
other fun things on Etsy:
TheEscapistArtist.Etsy.Com

RIOT GRRRL PRESS MARCH 2020

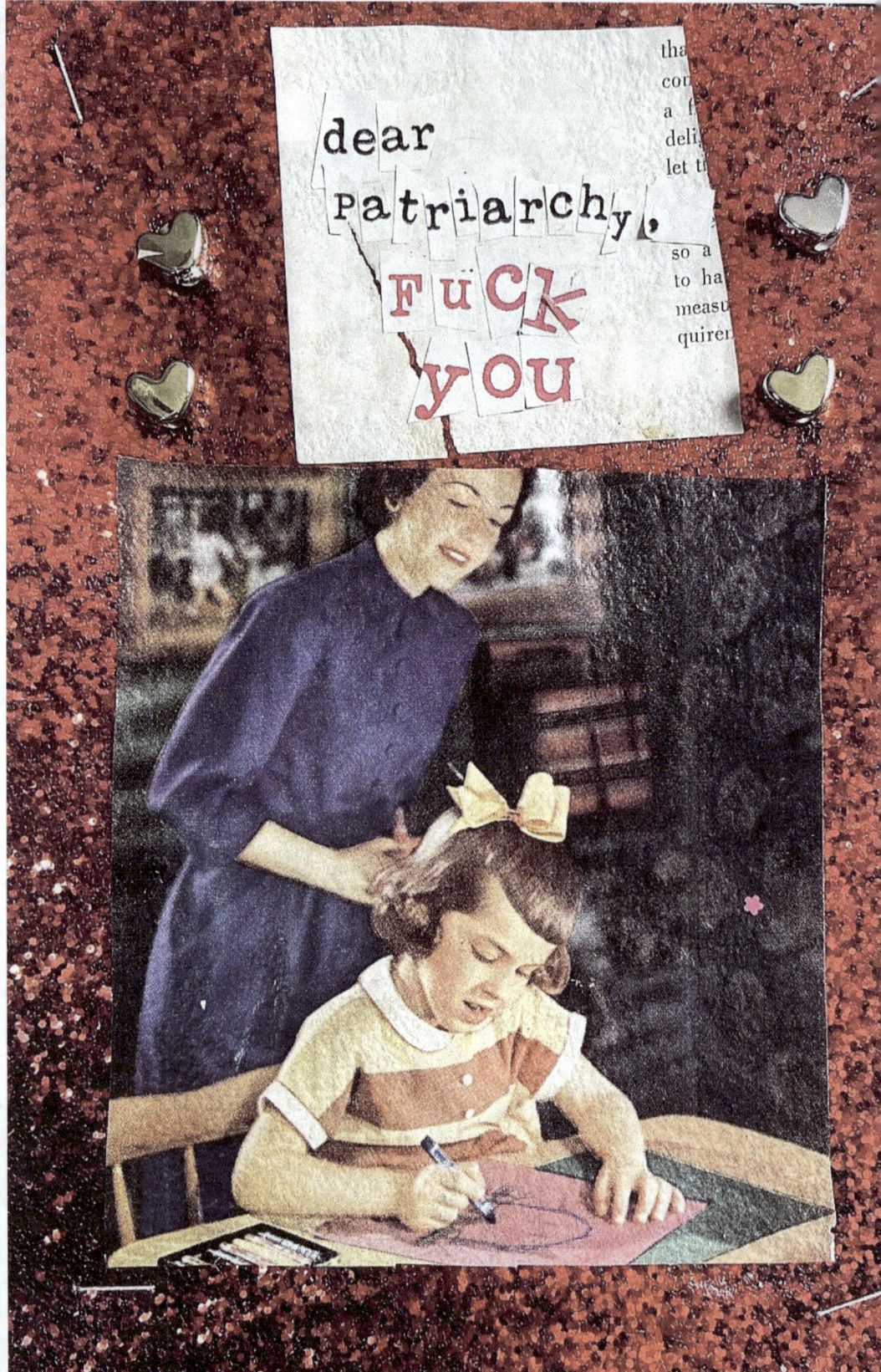

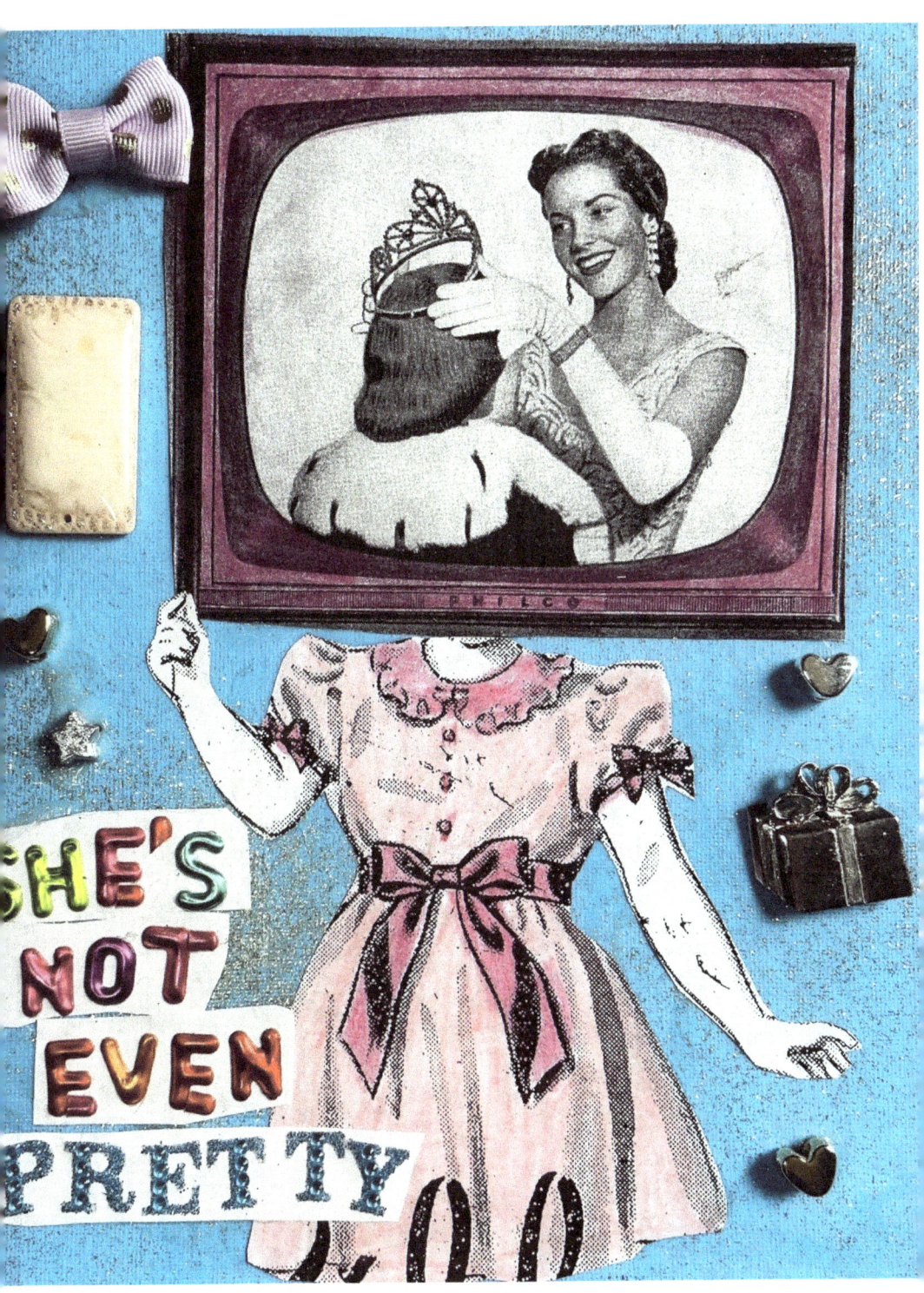

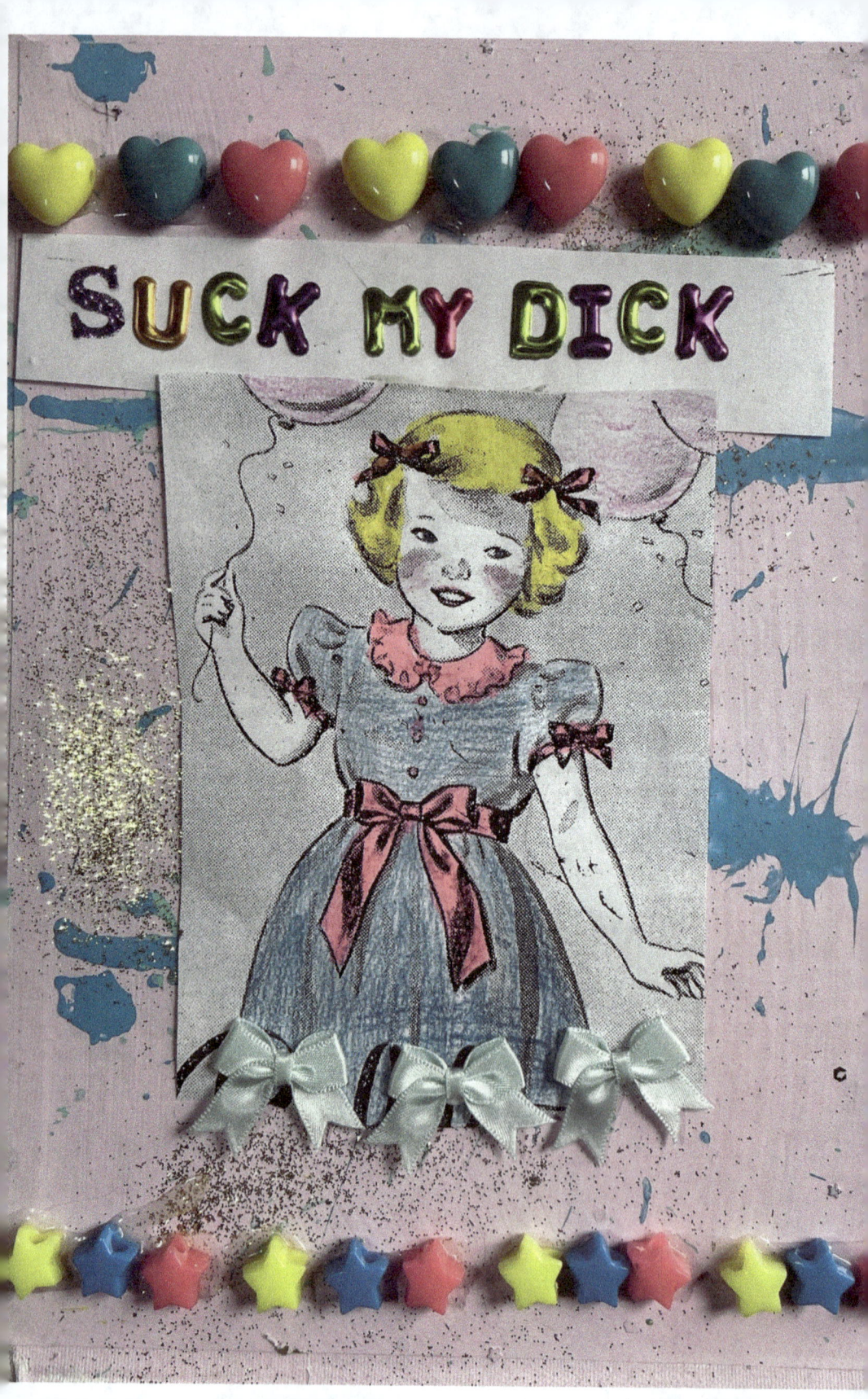

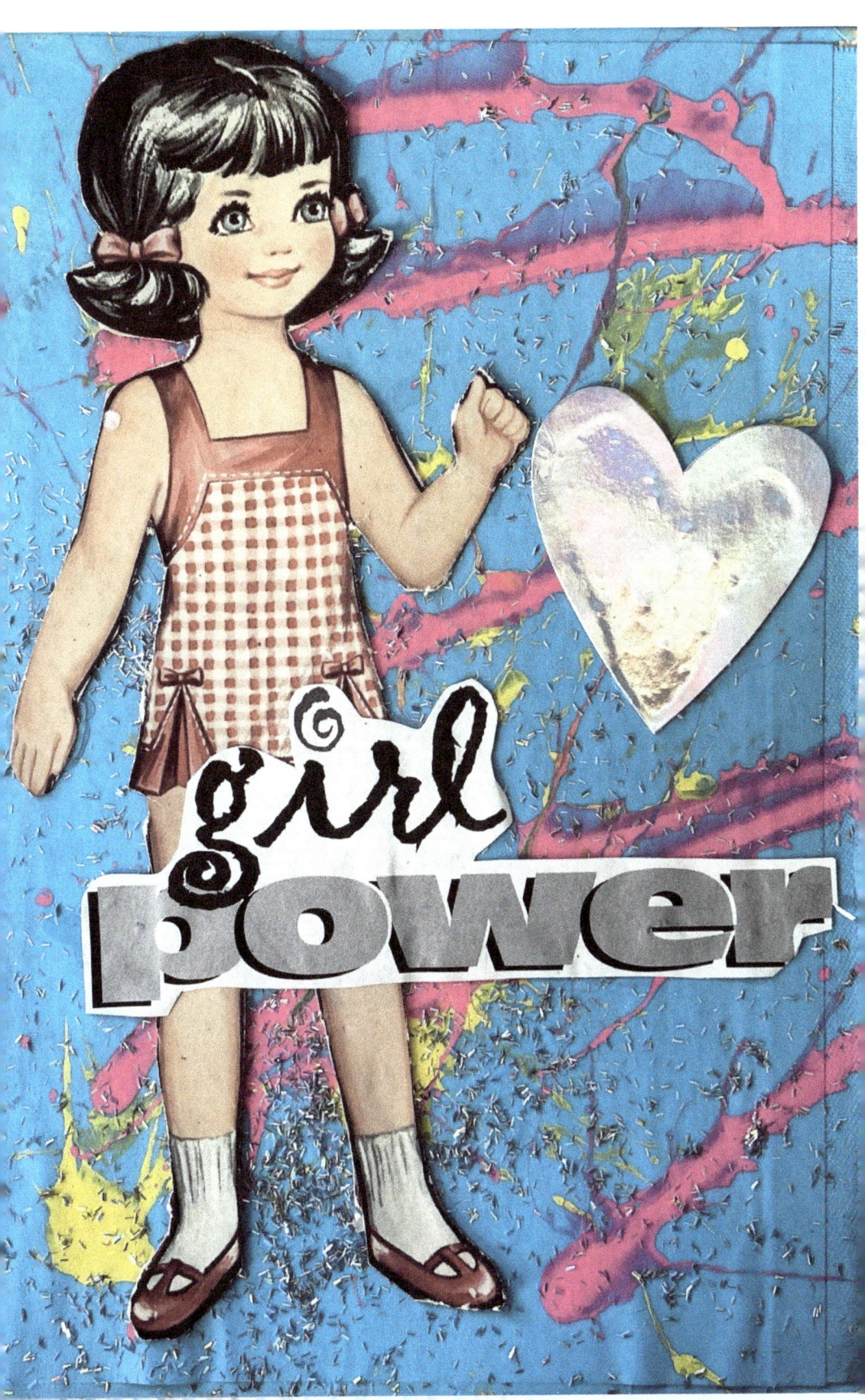

girl power

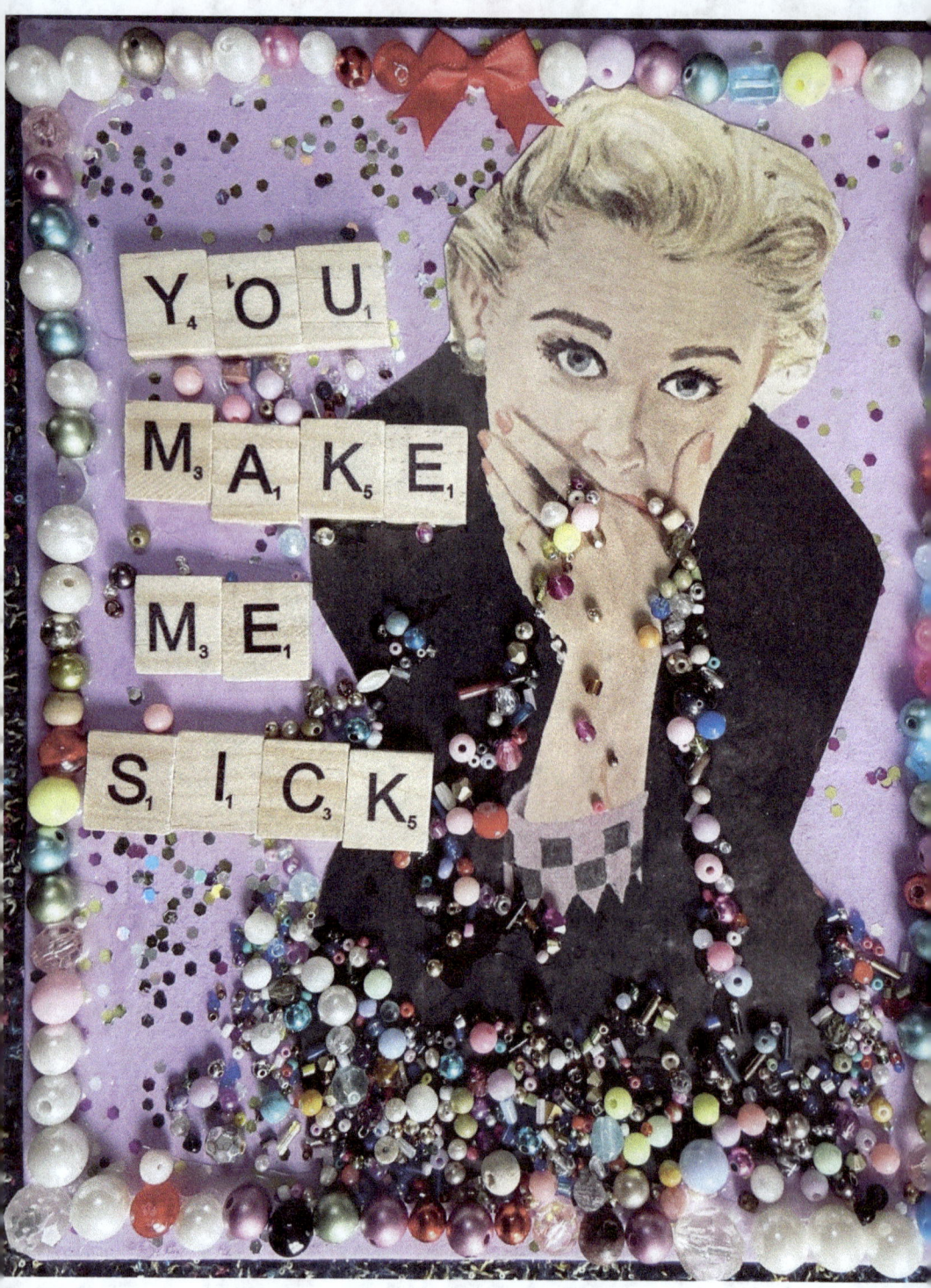

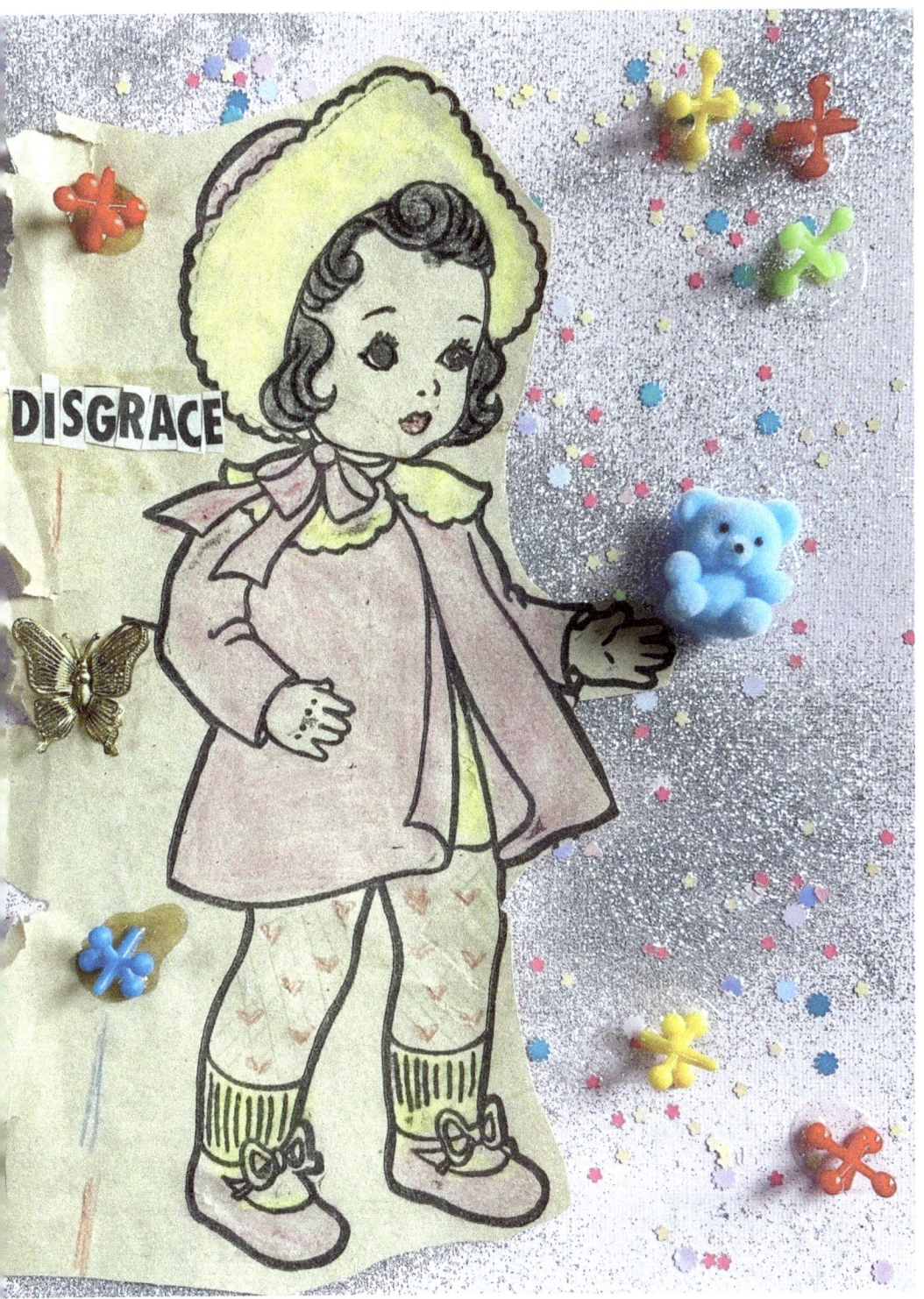

DISGRACE

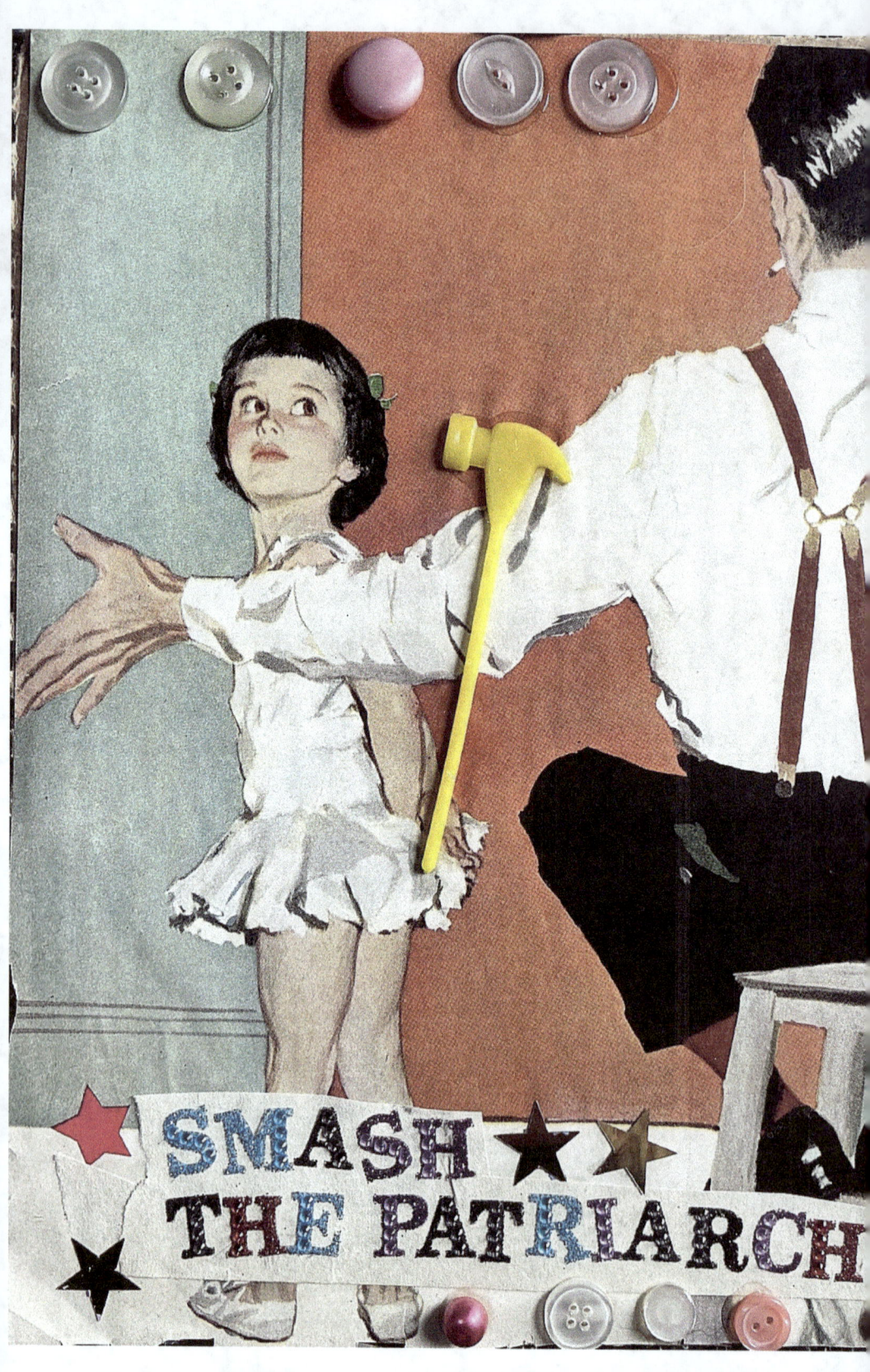

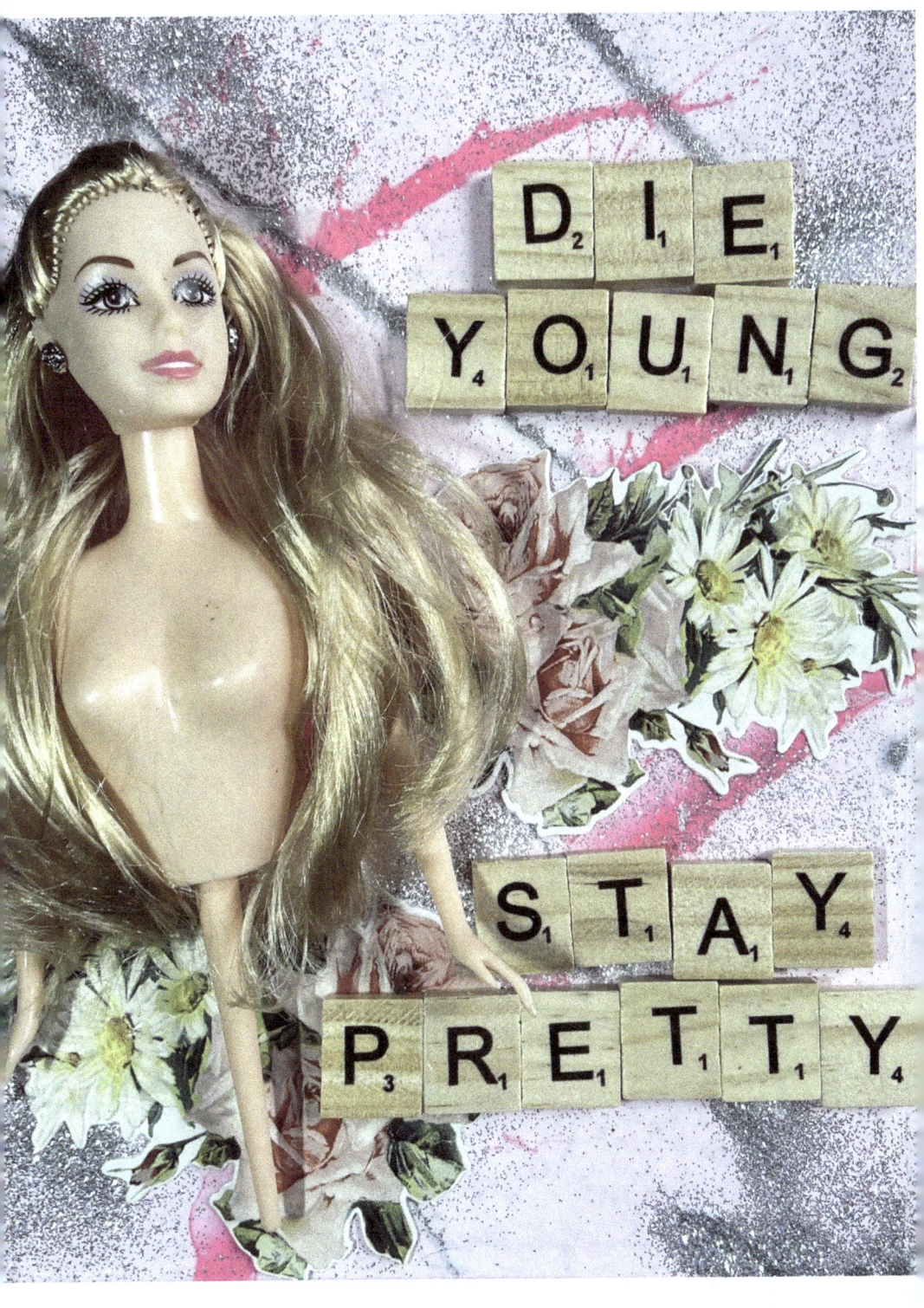

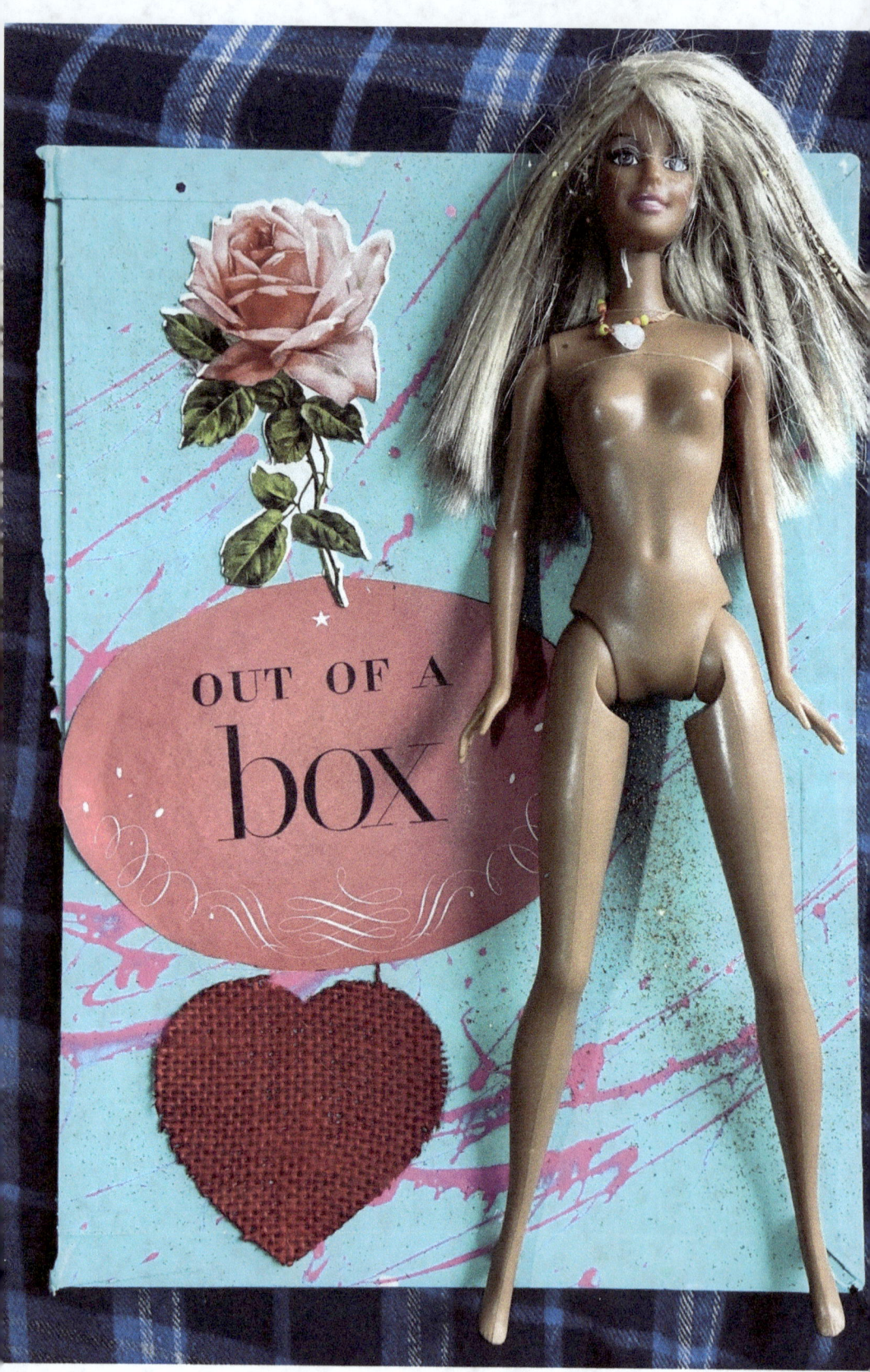

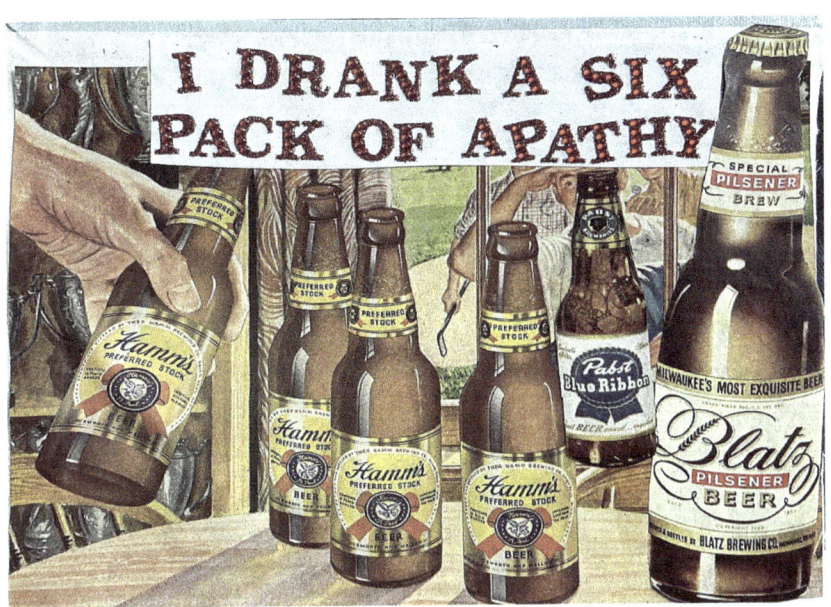

I DRANK A SIX PACK OF APATHY

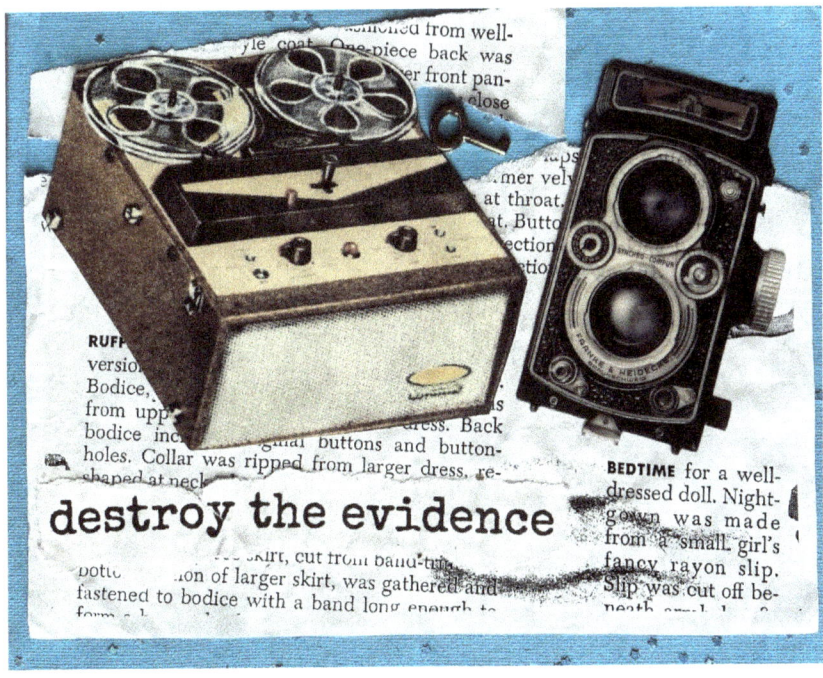

destroy the evidence

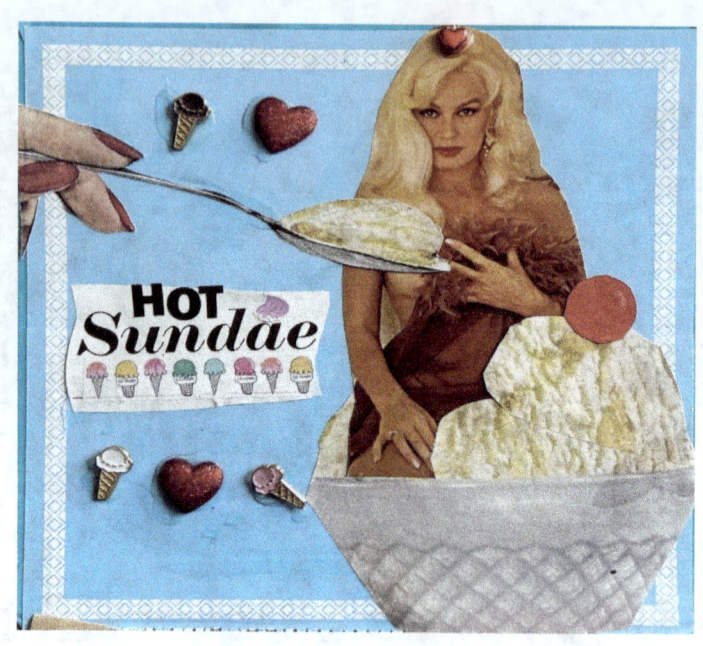

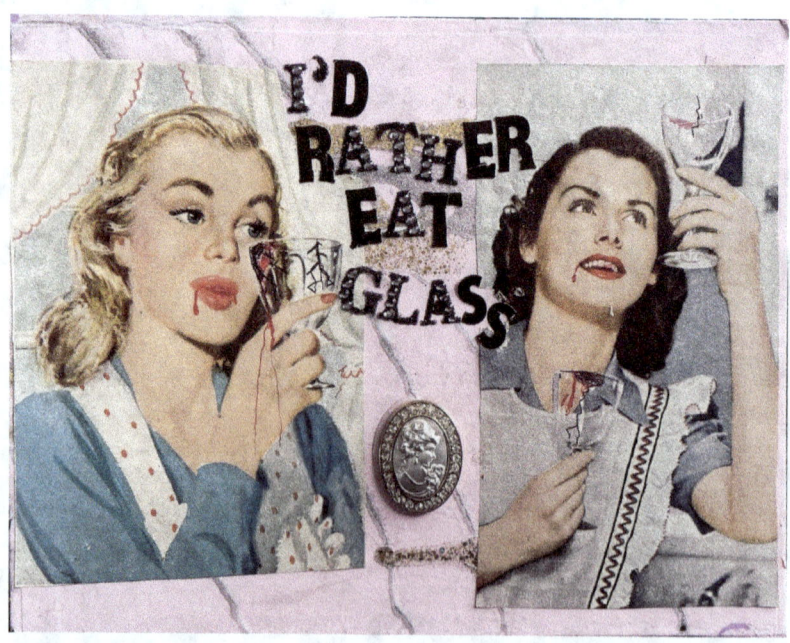

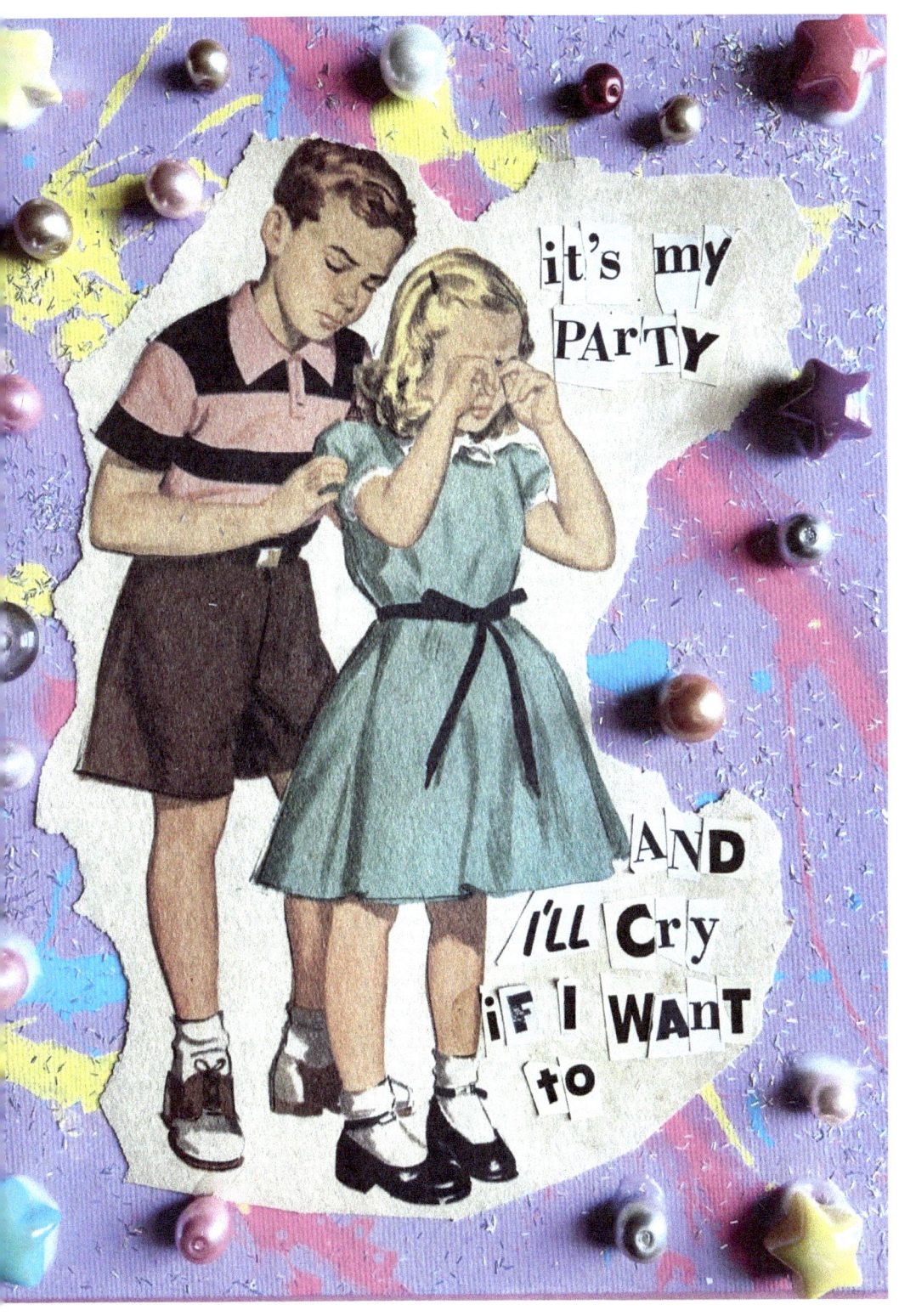

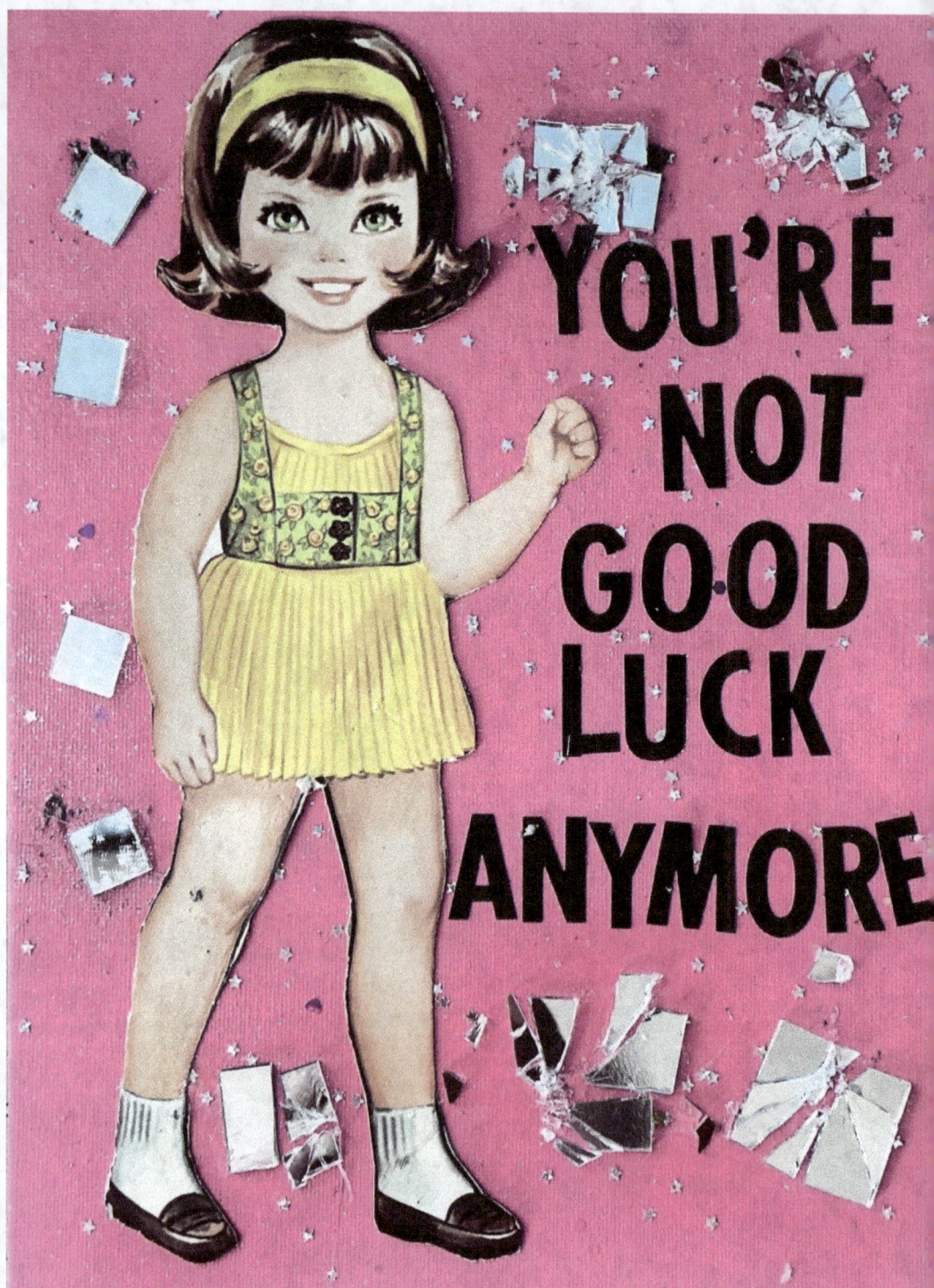

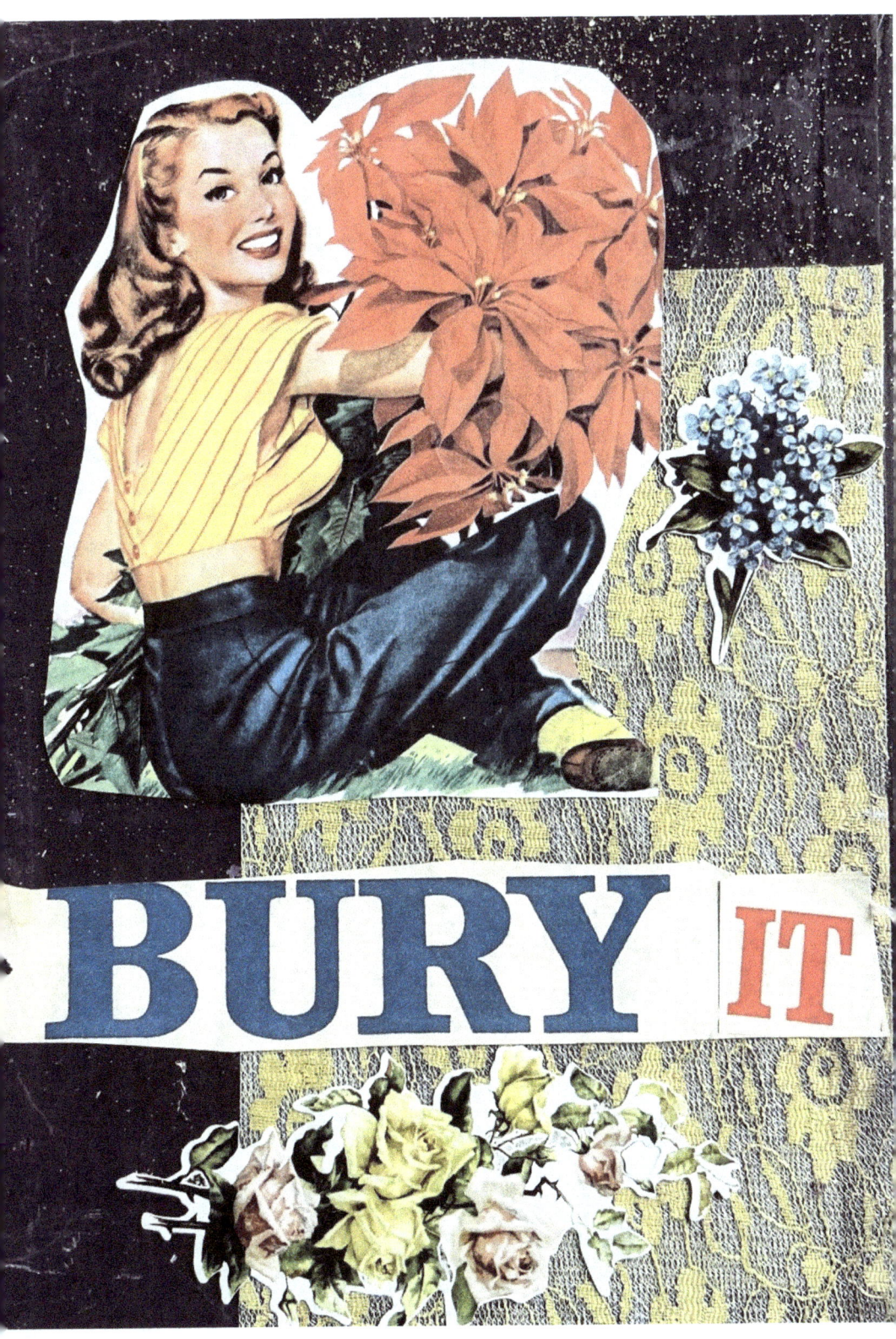

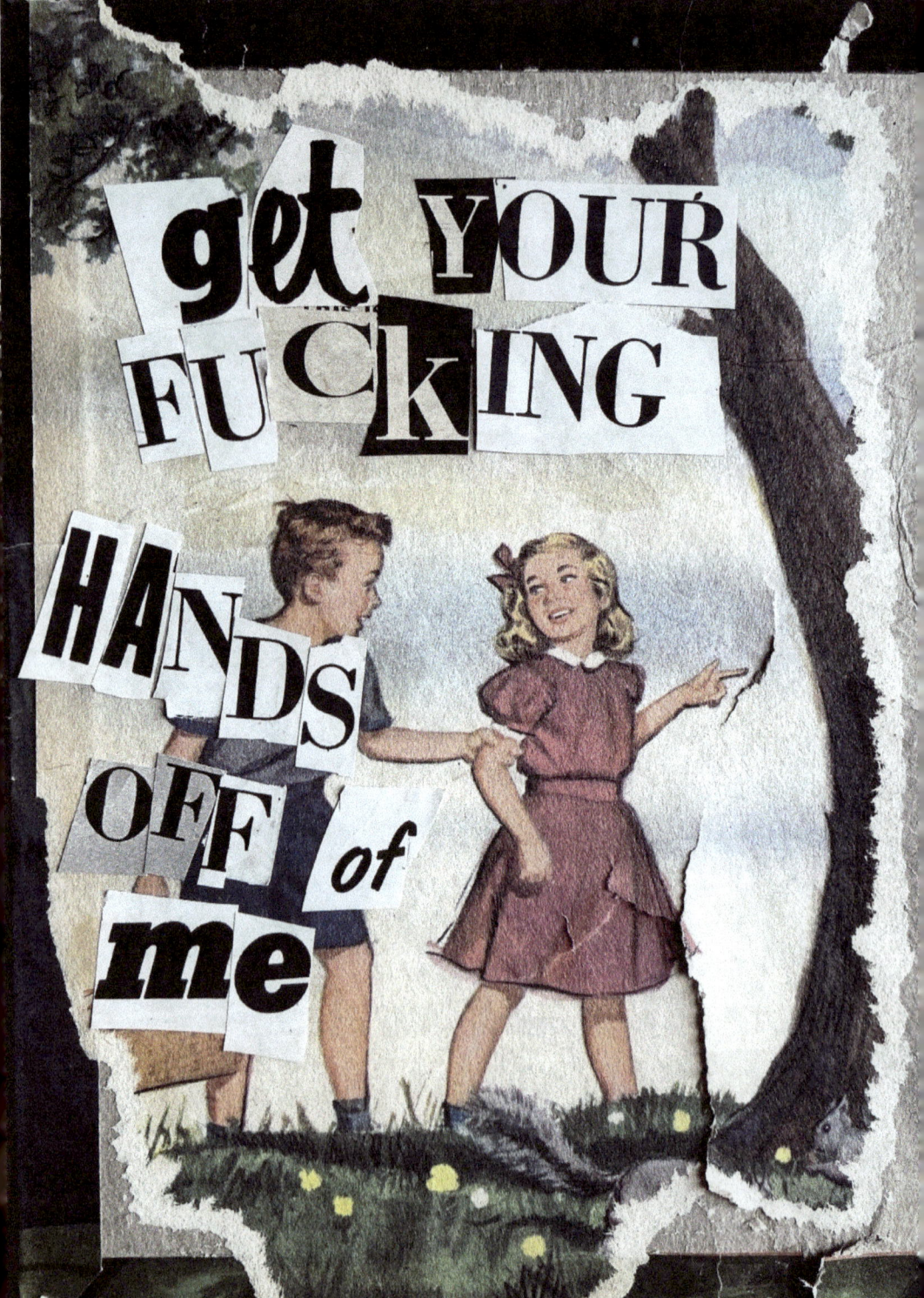

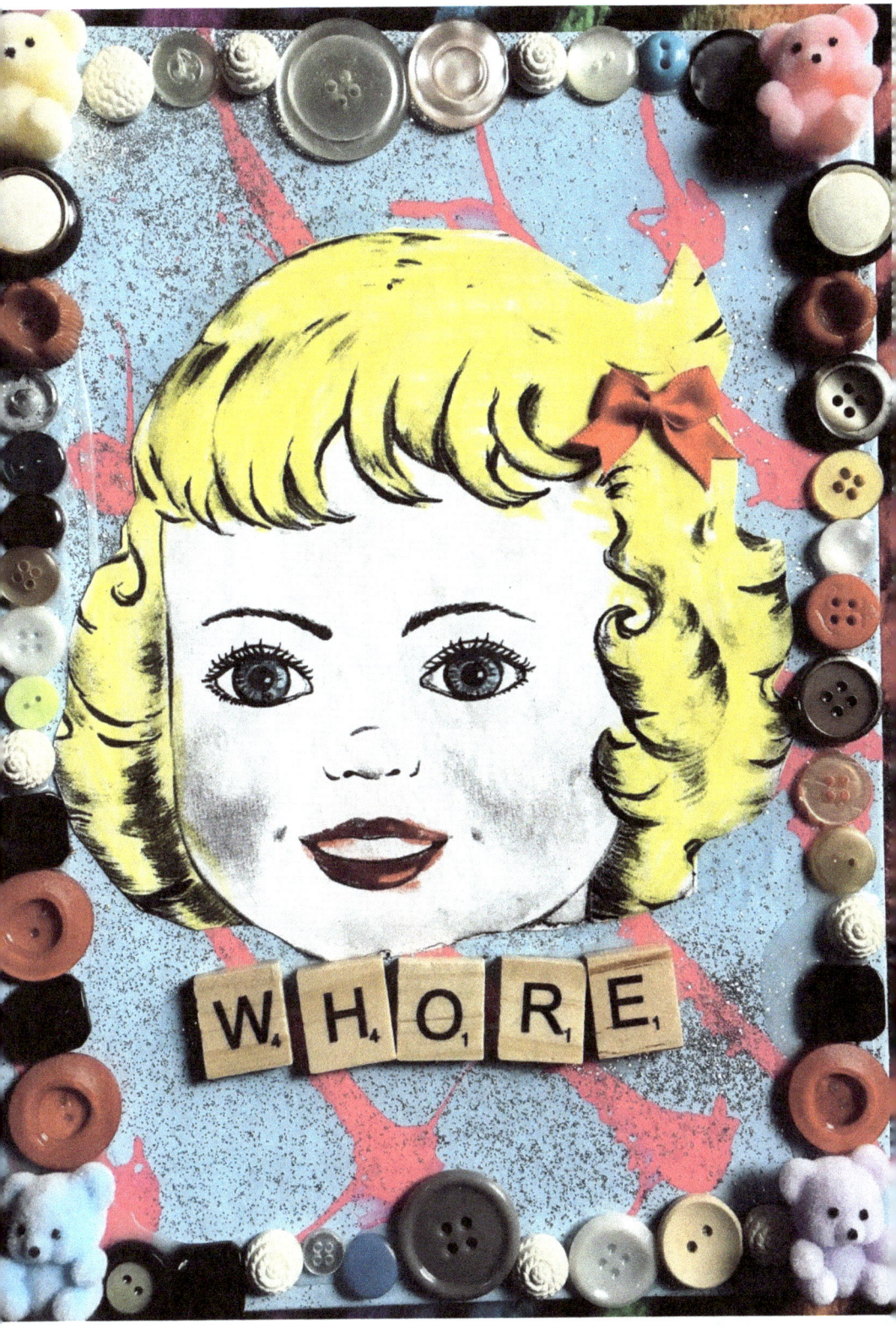

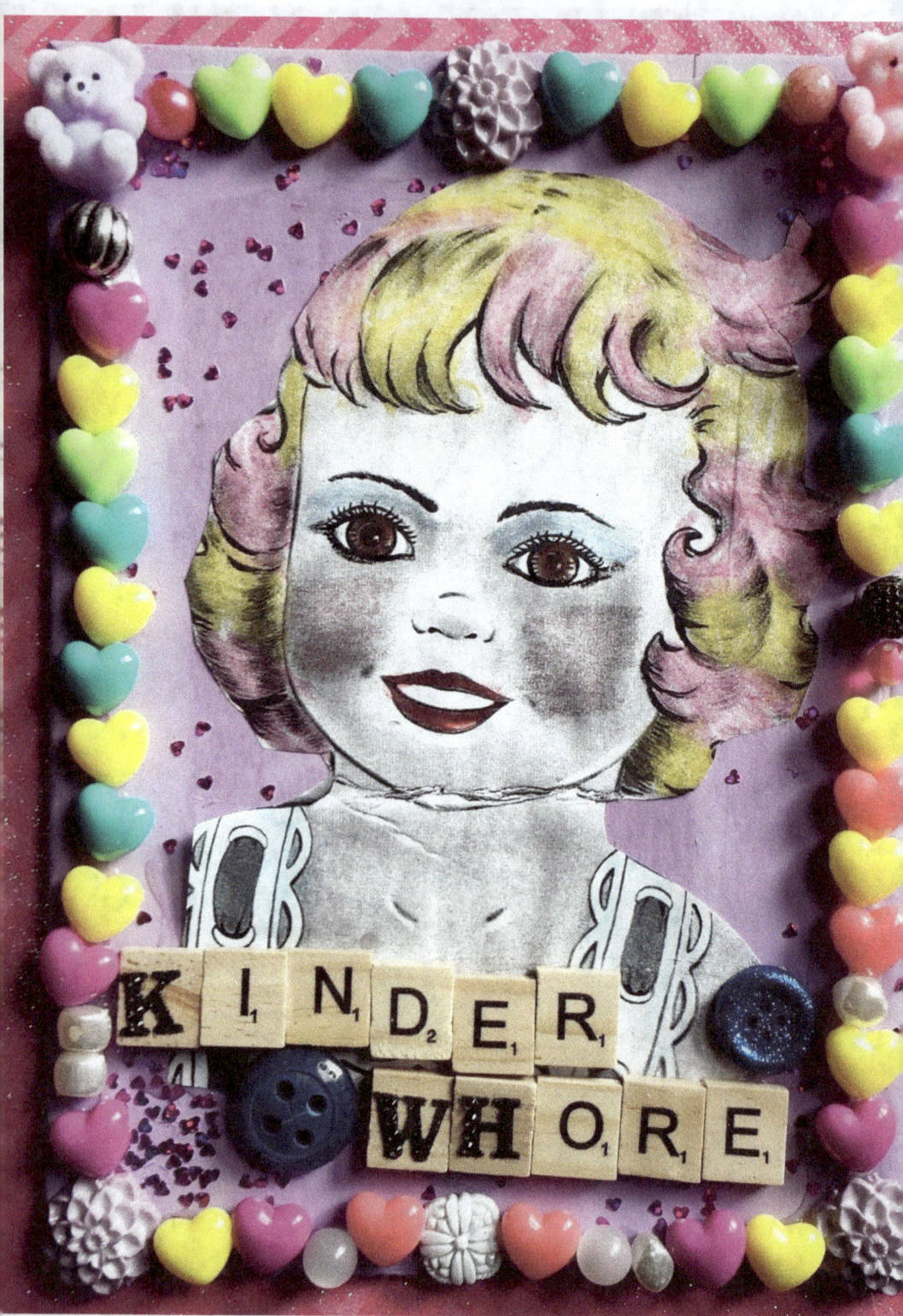

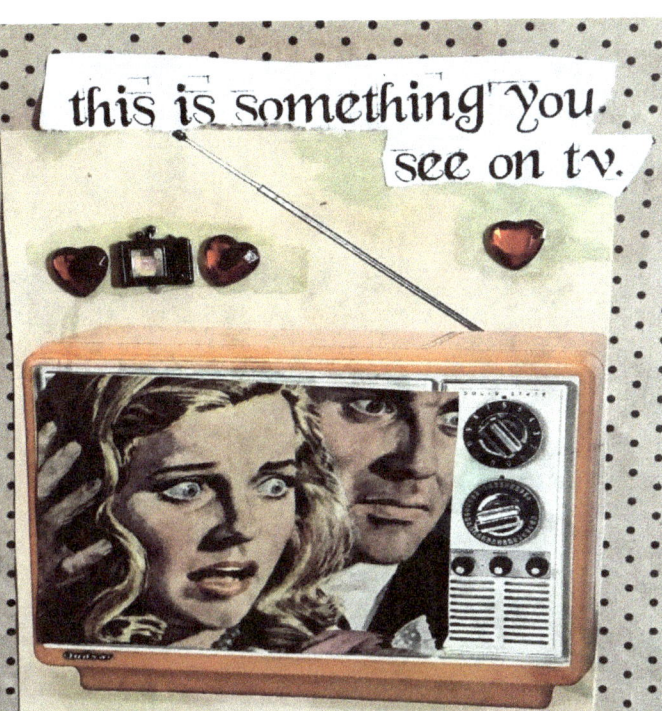

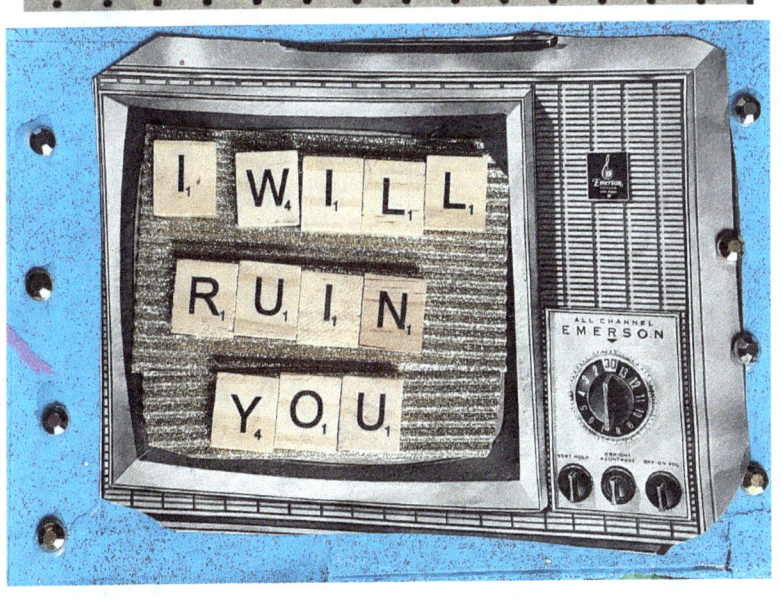

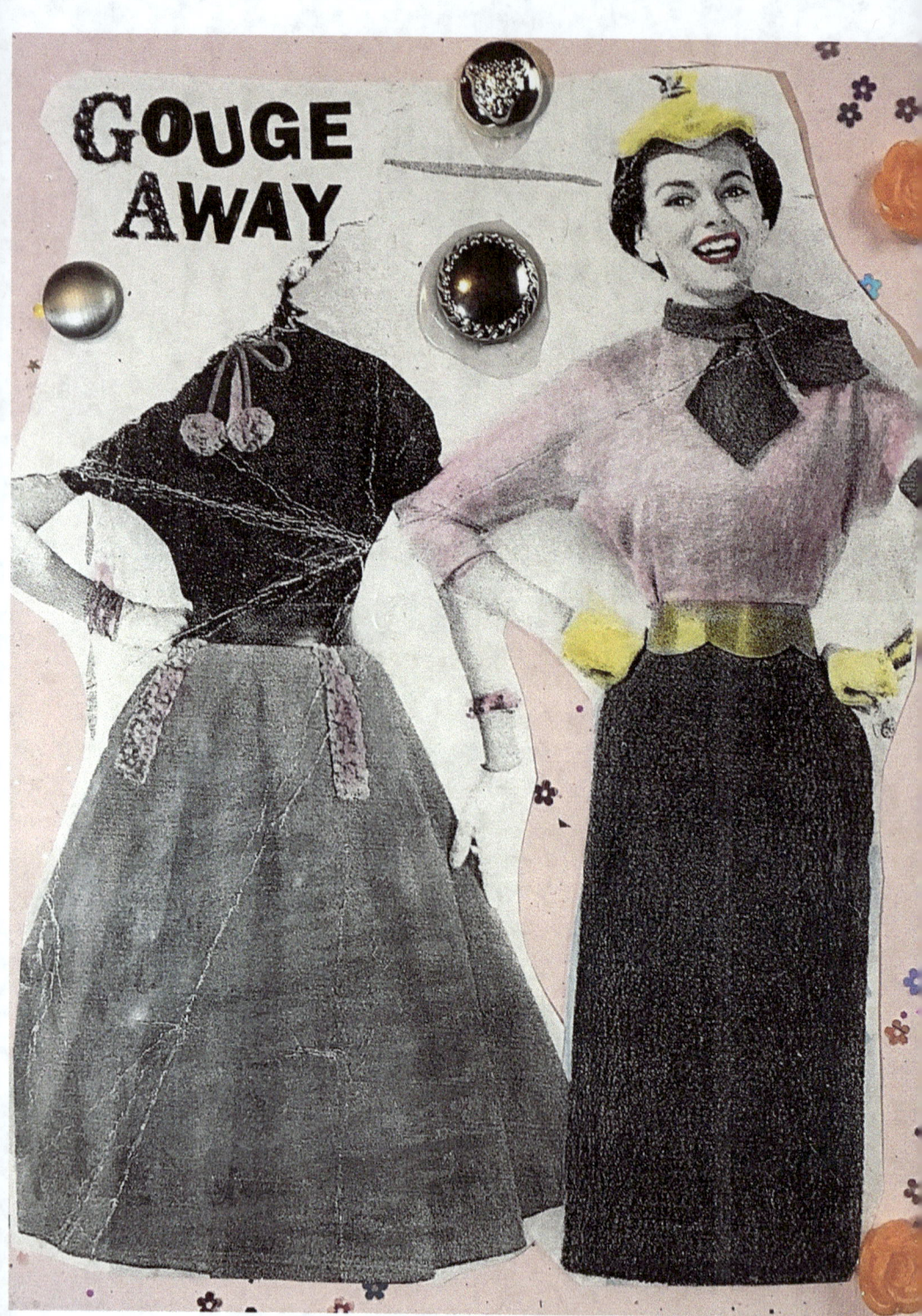

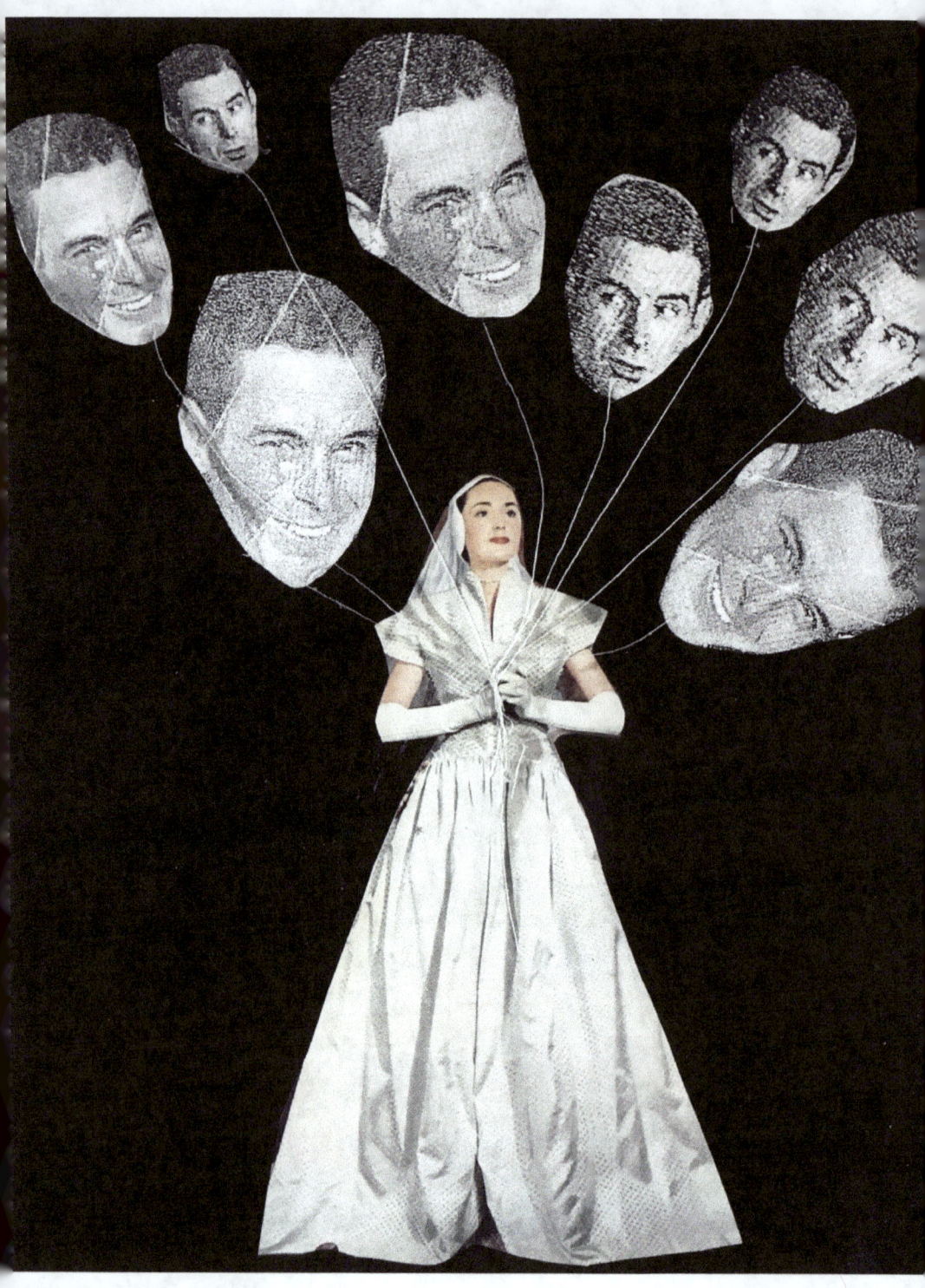

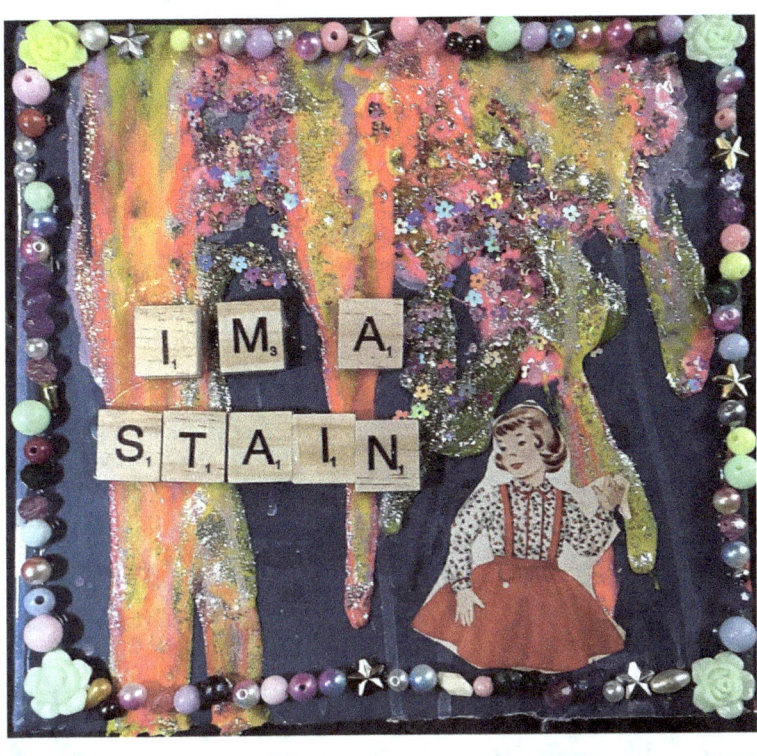

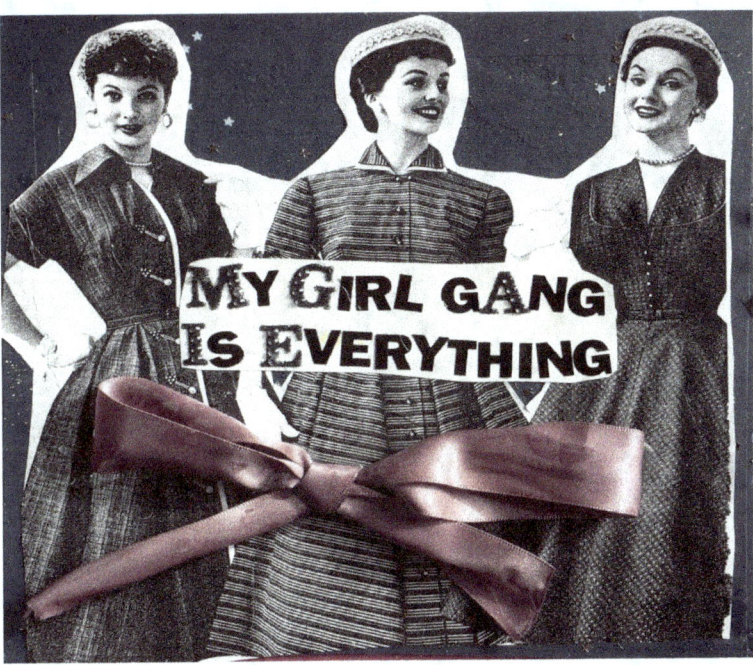

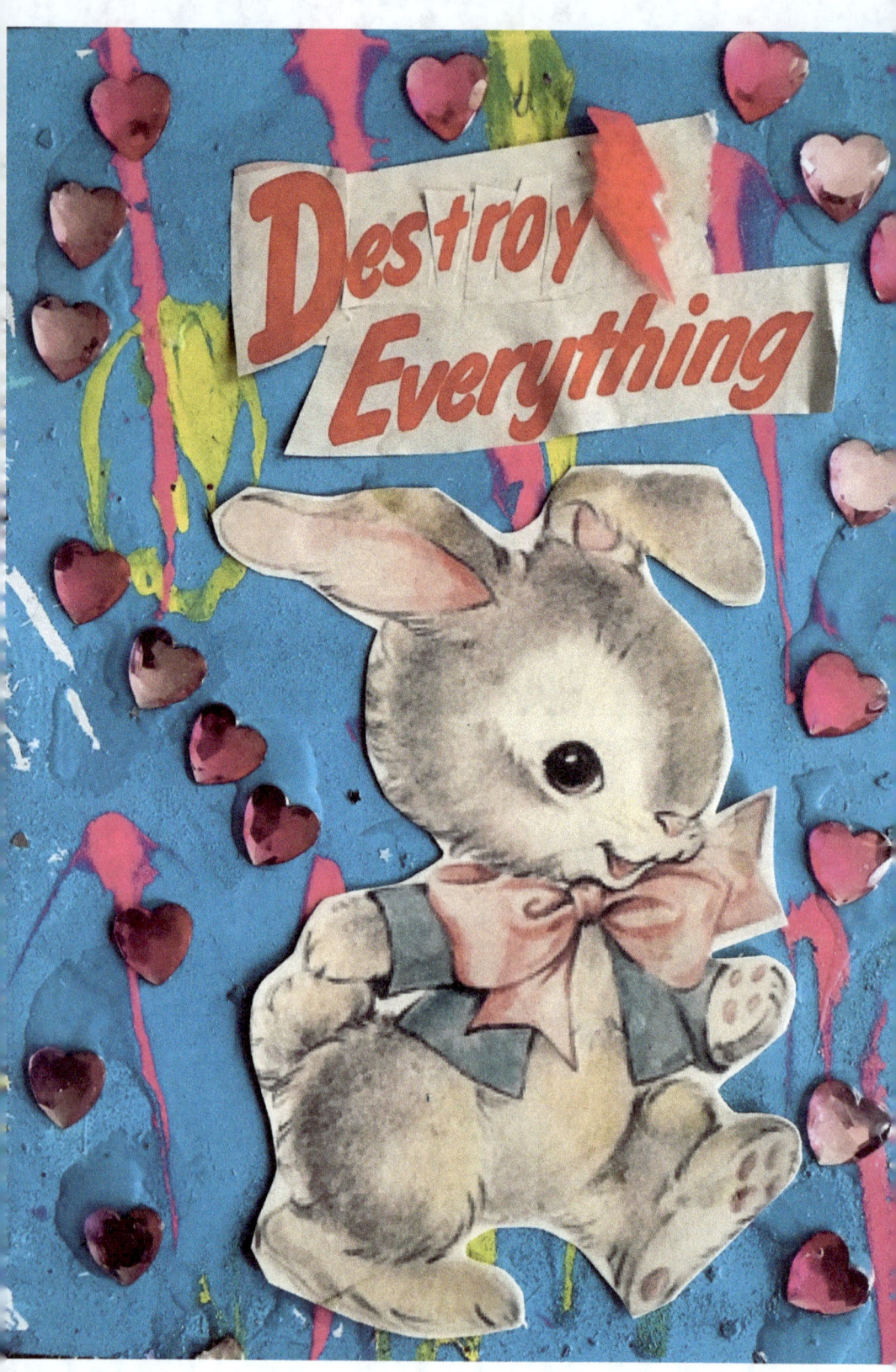

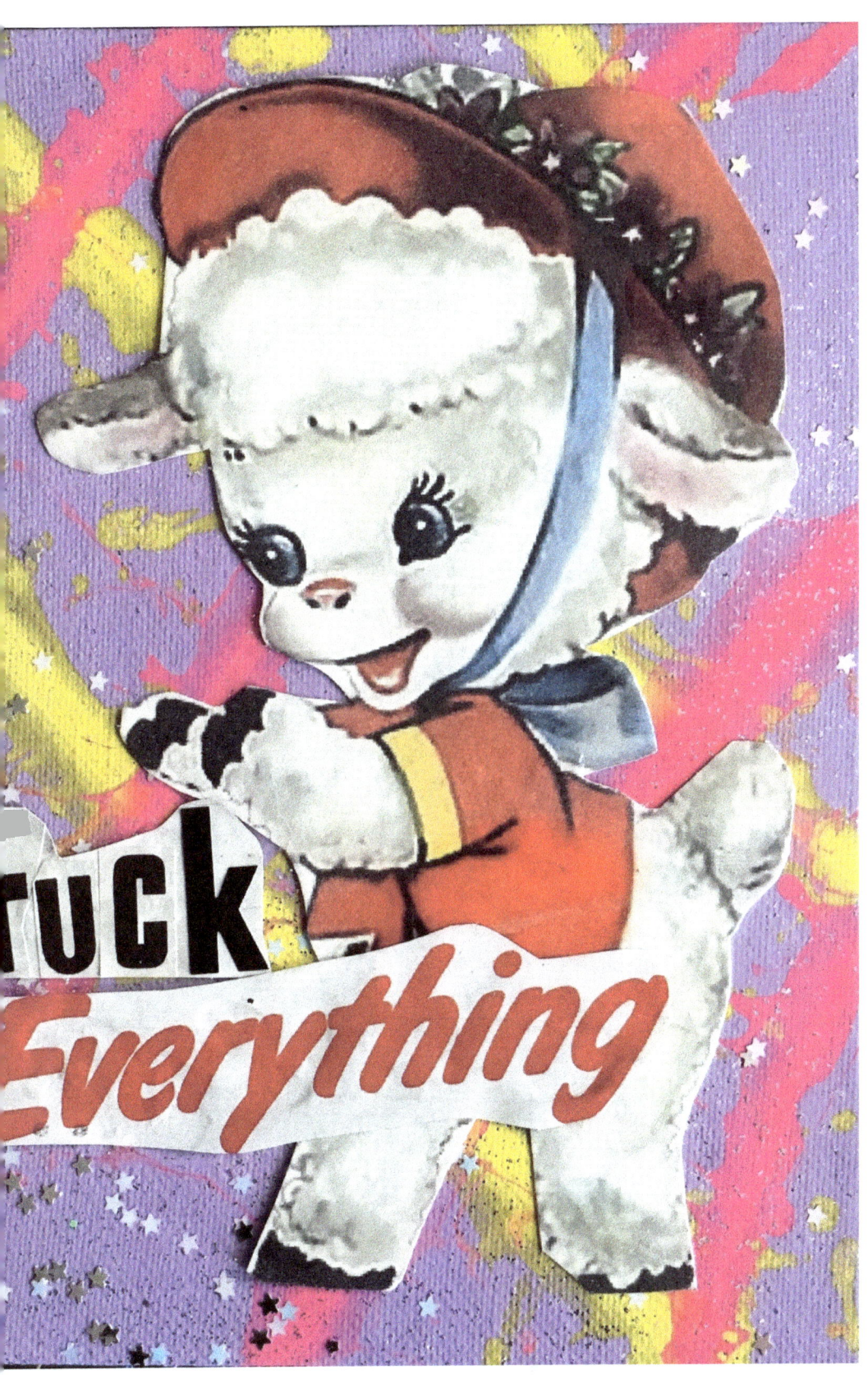

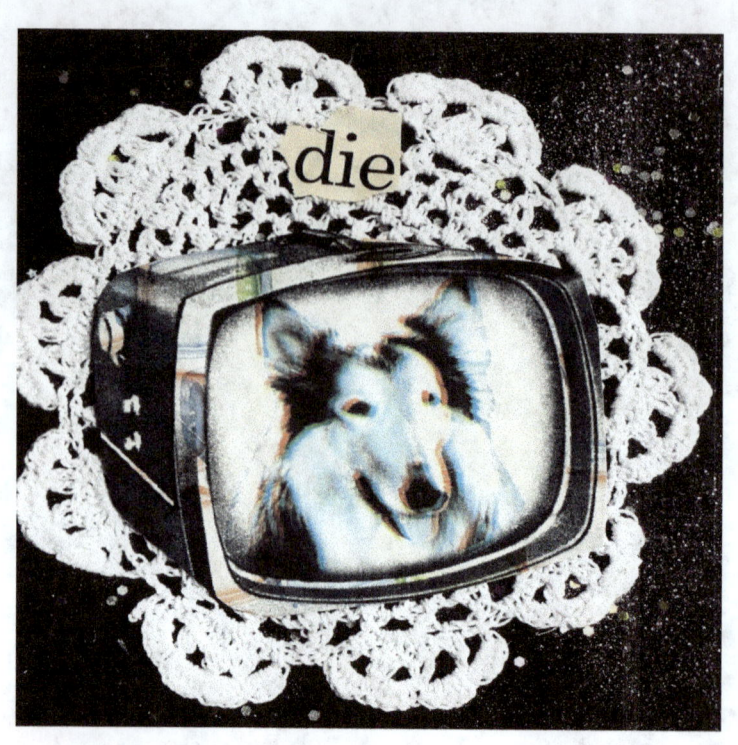

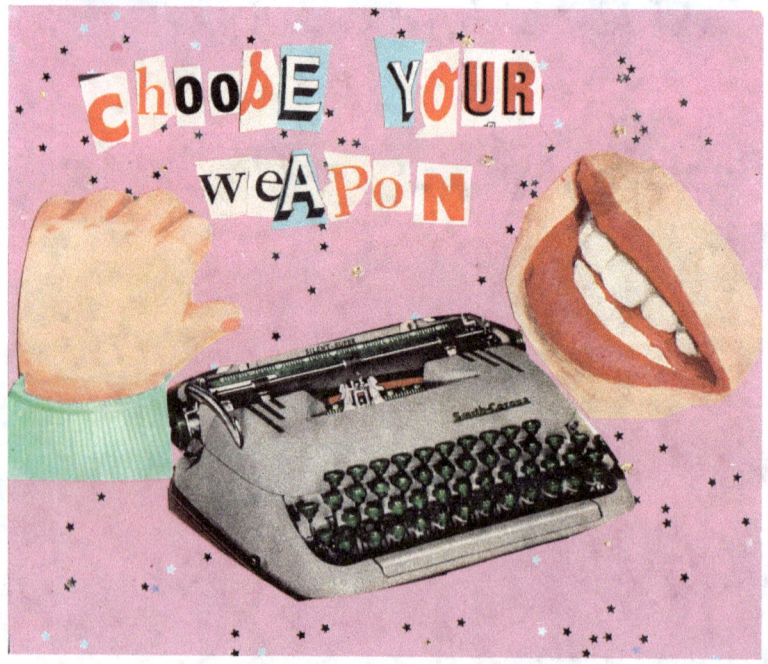

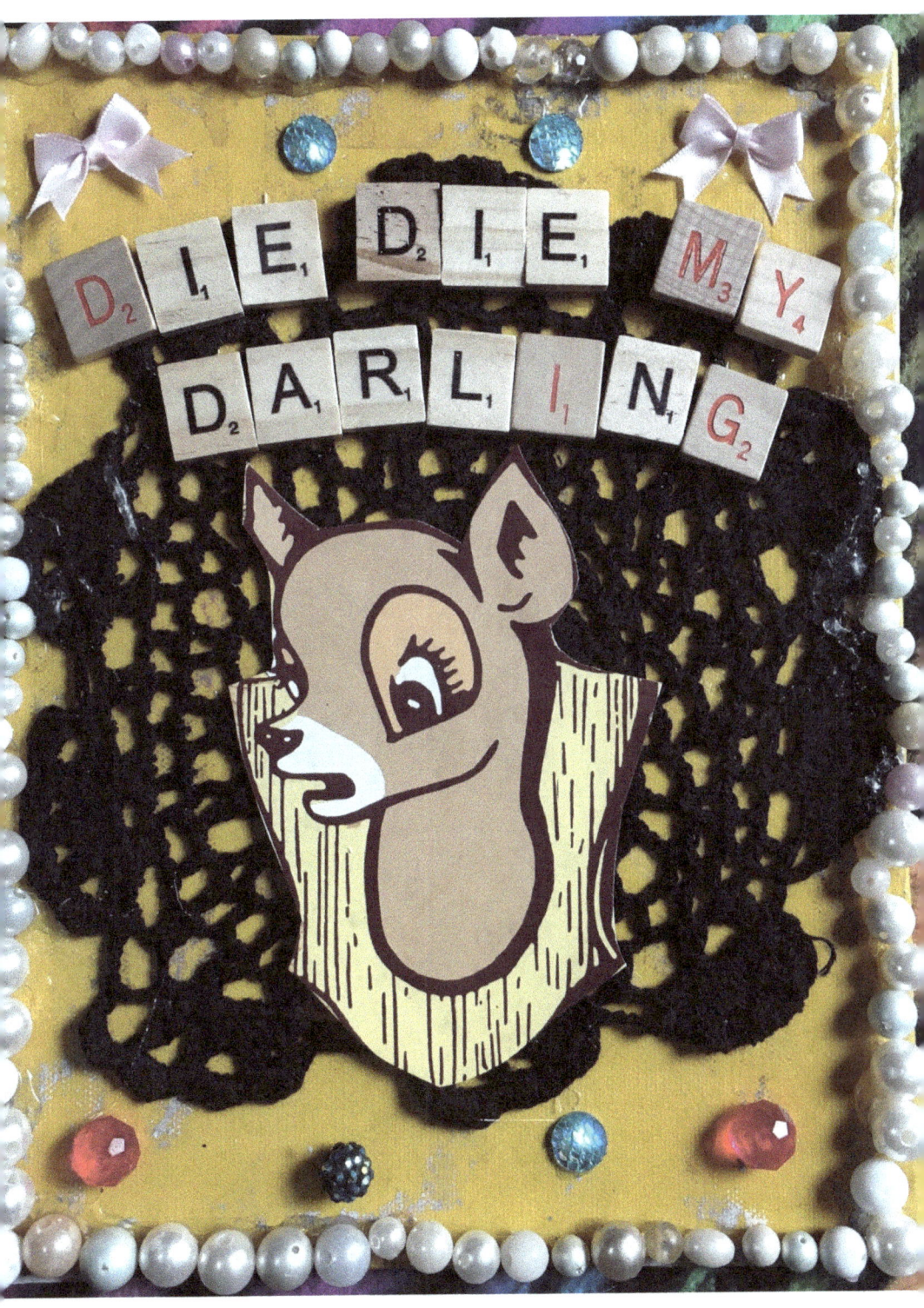

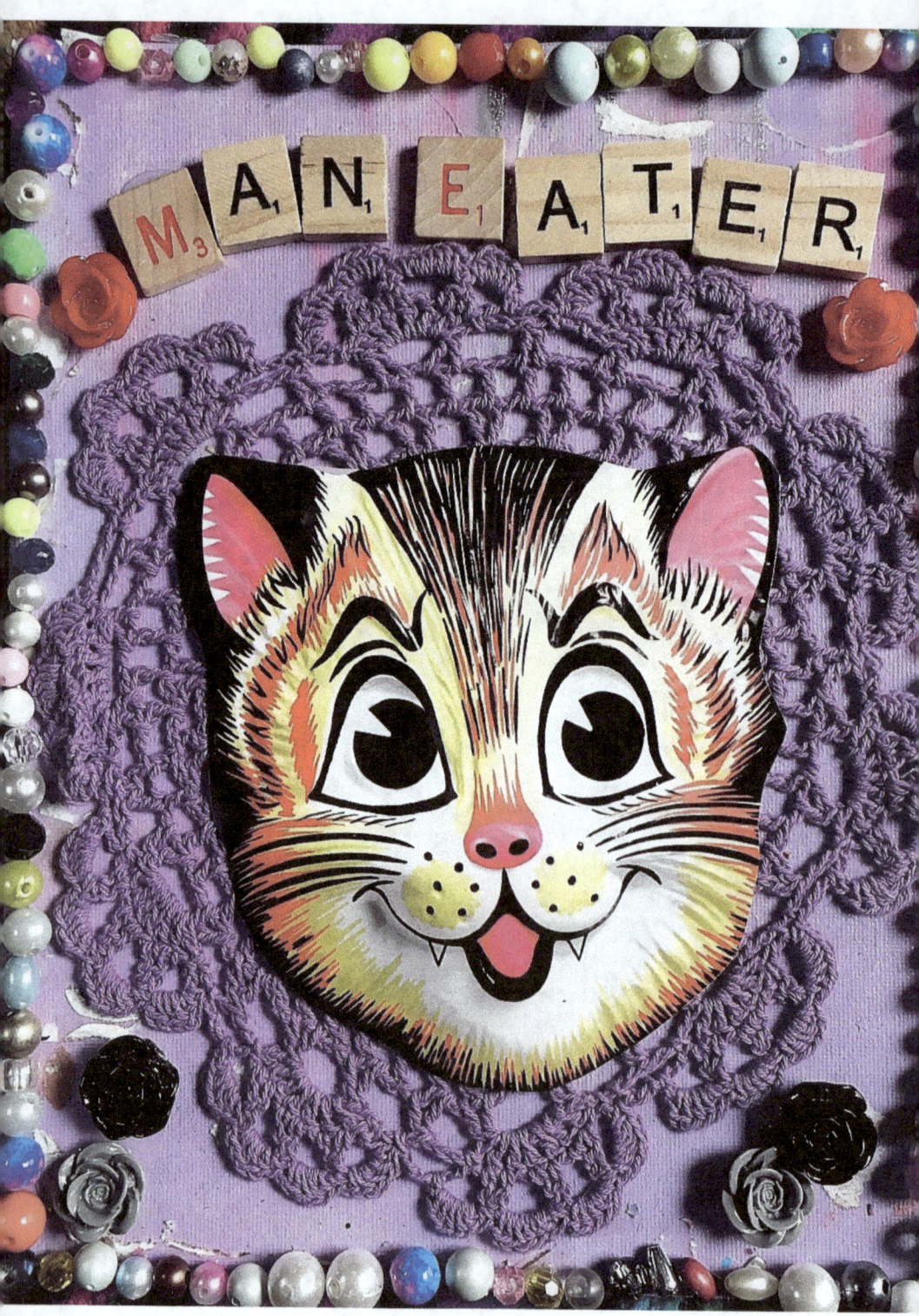

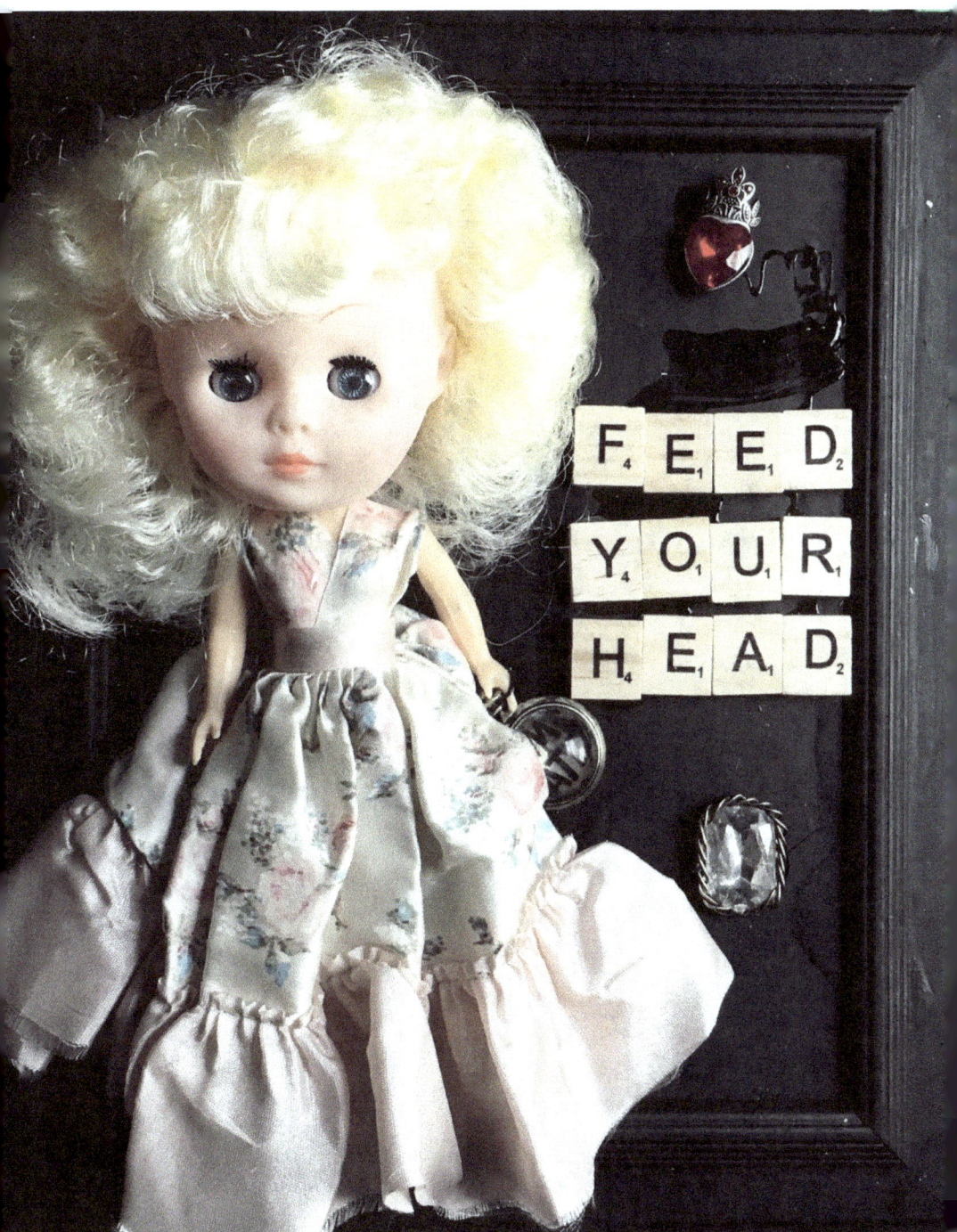

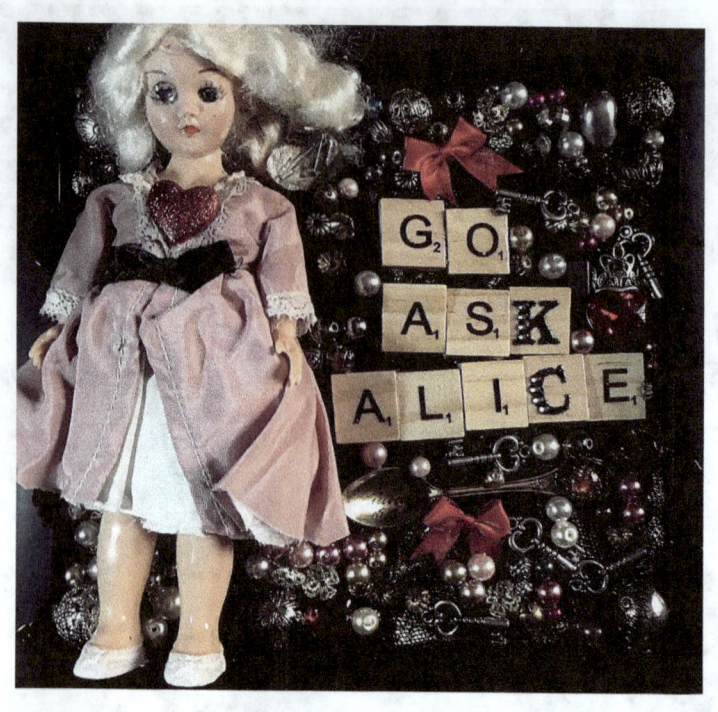

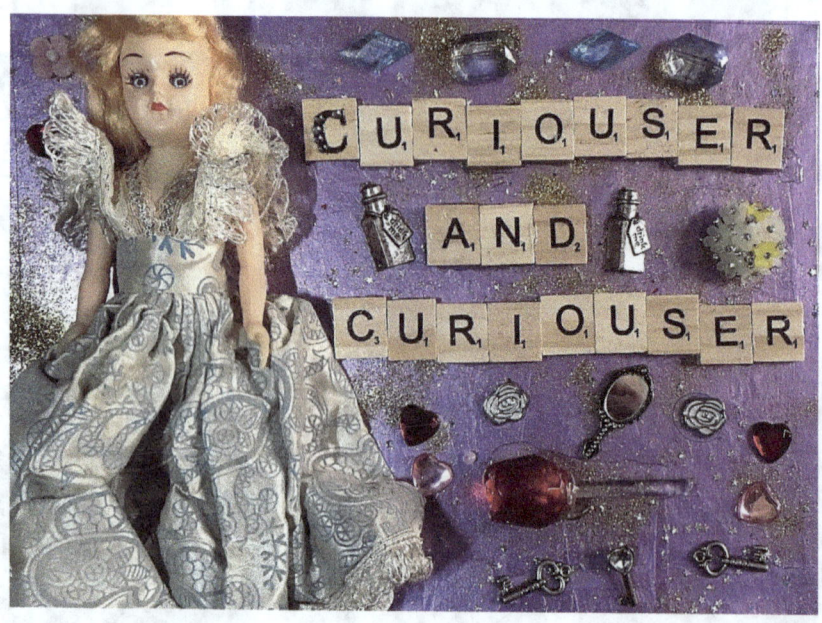

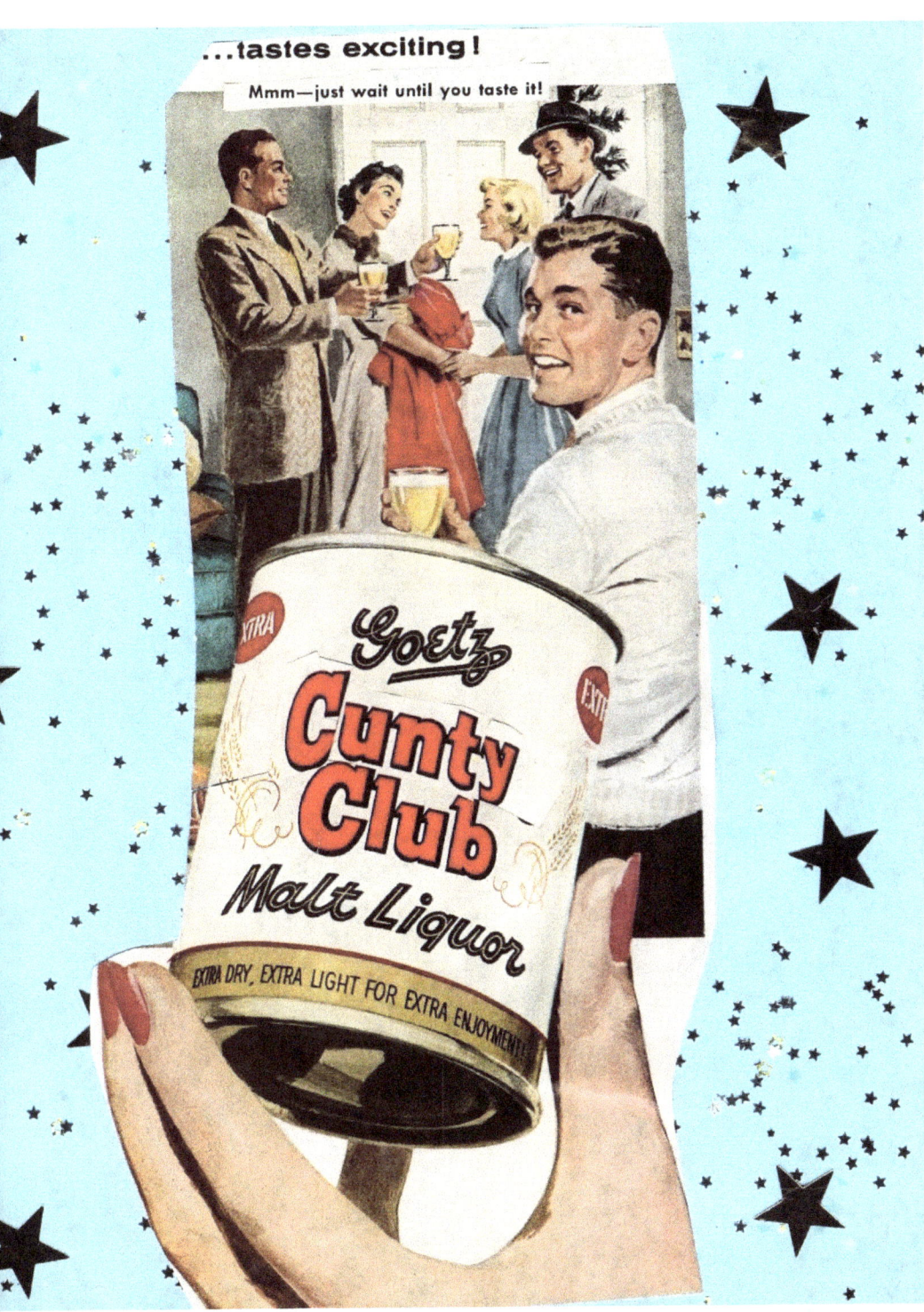

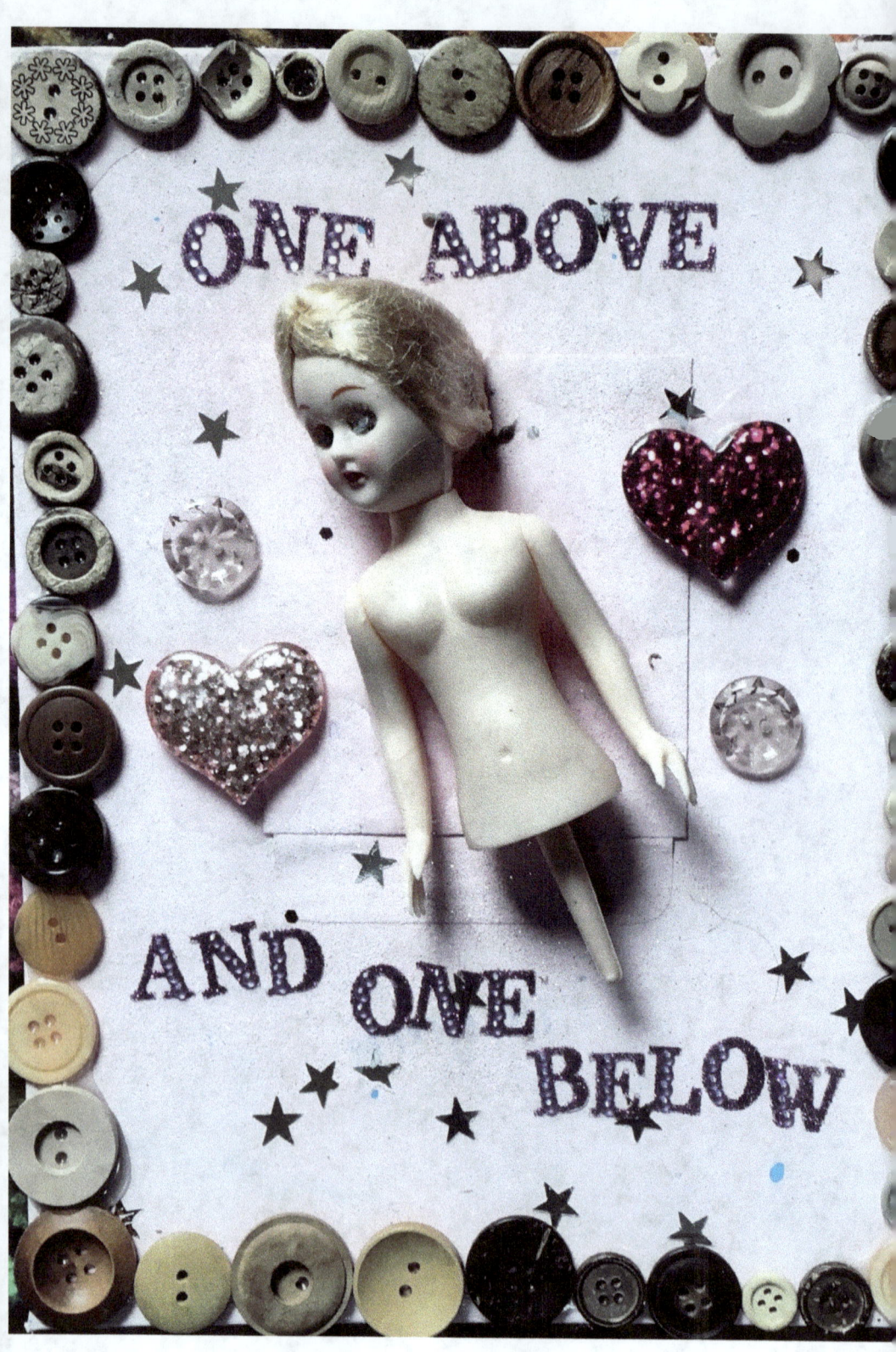

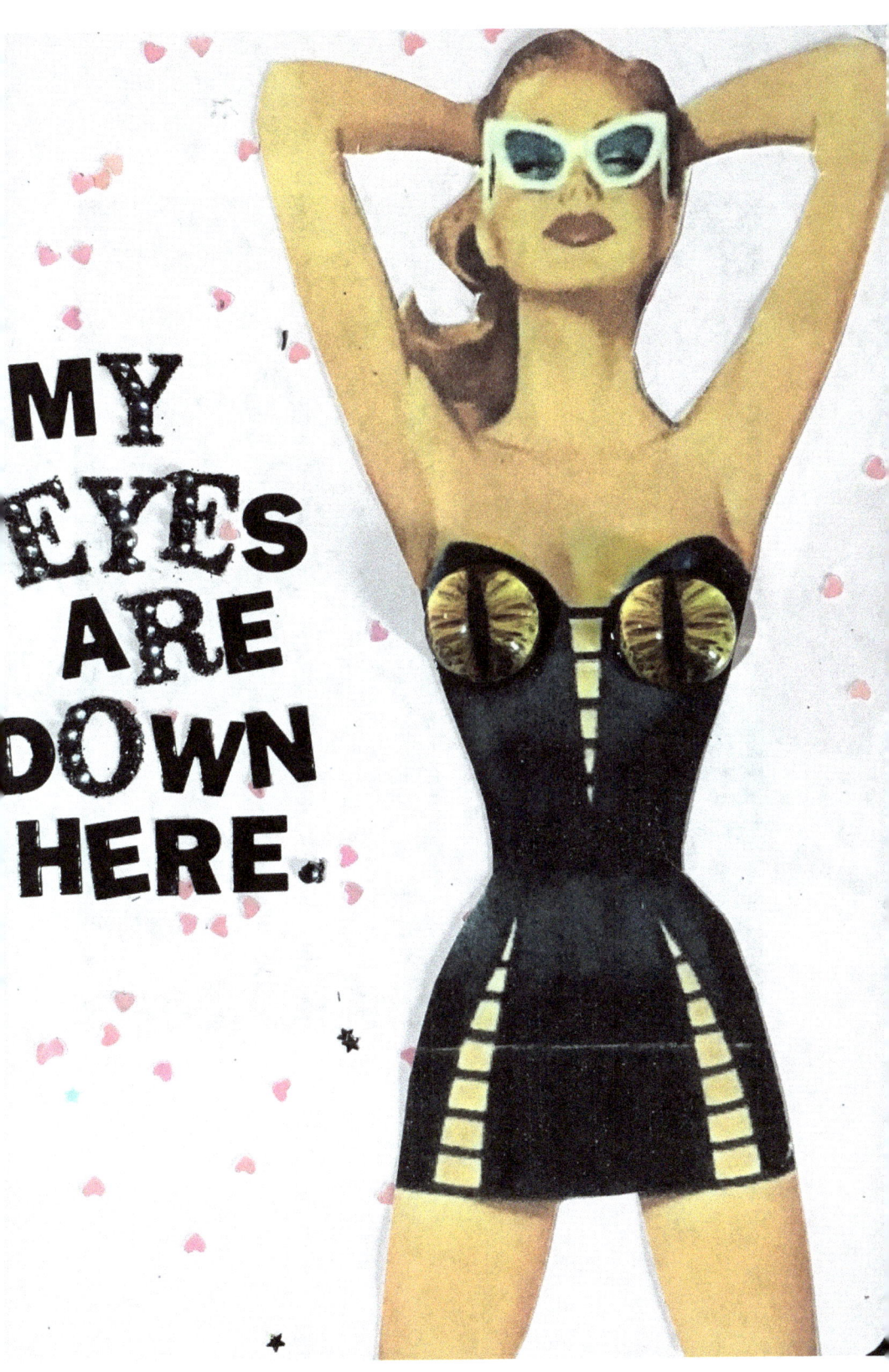

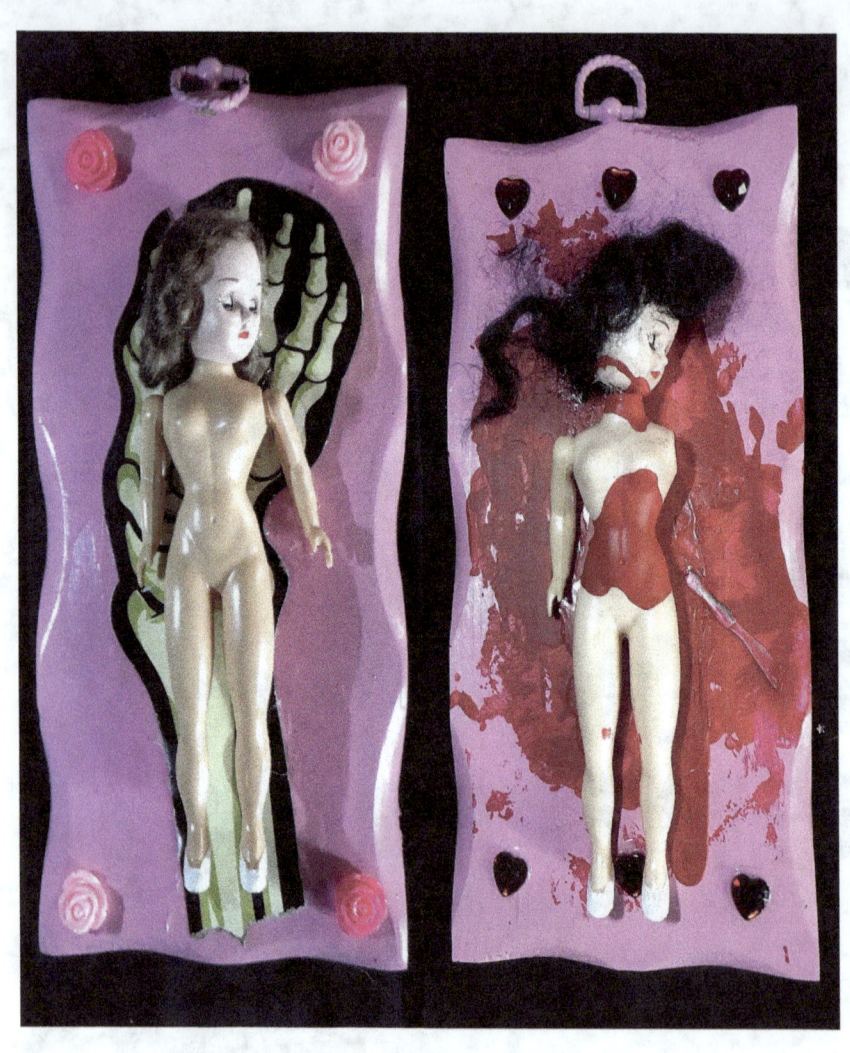

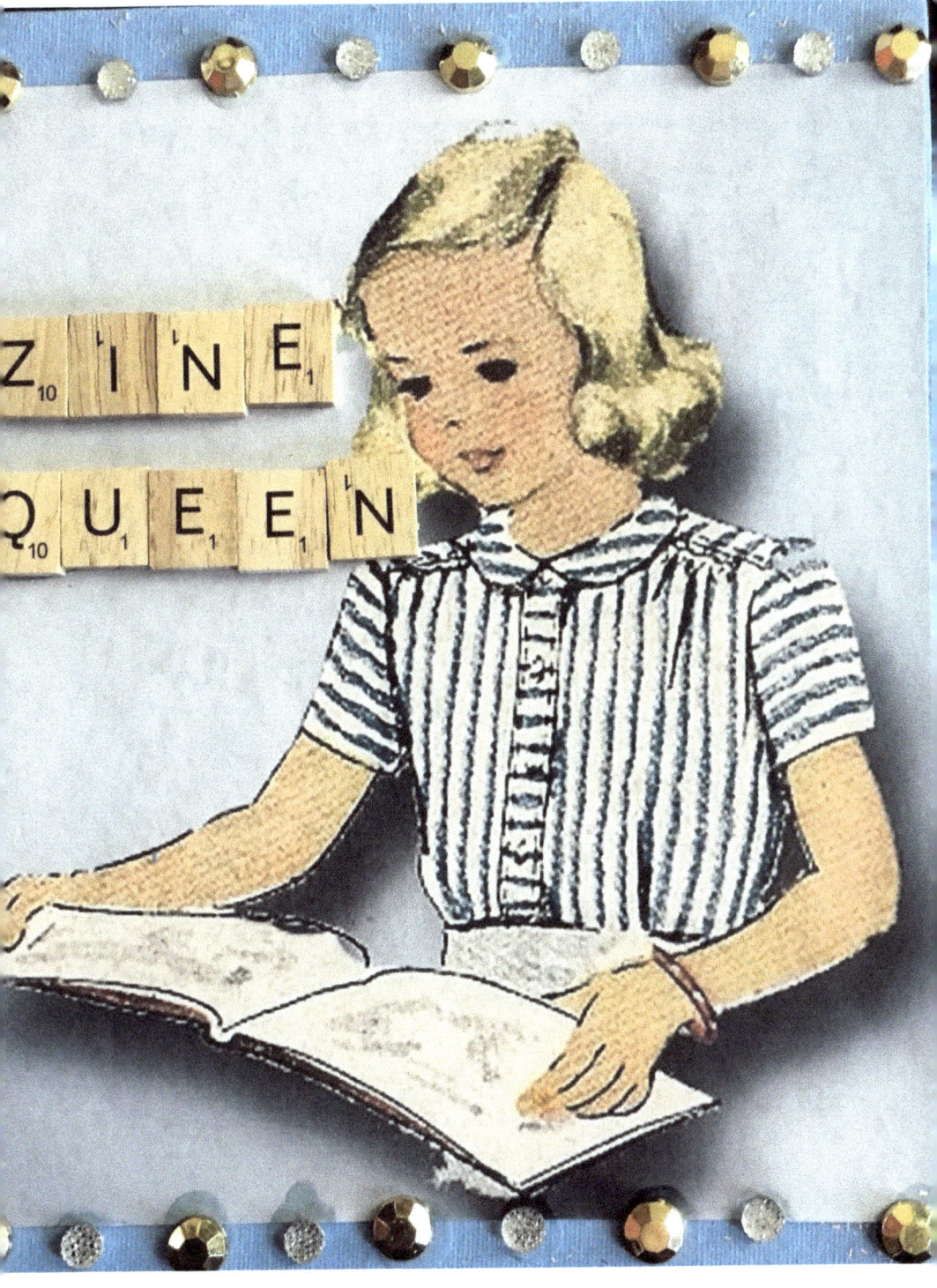

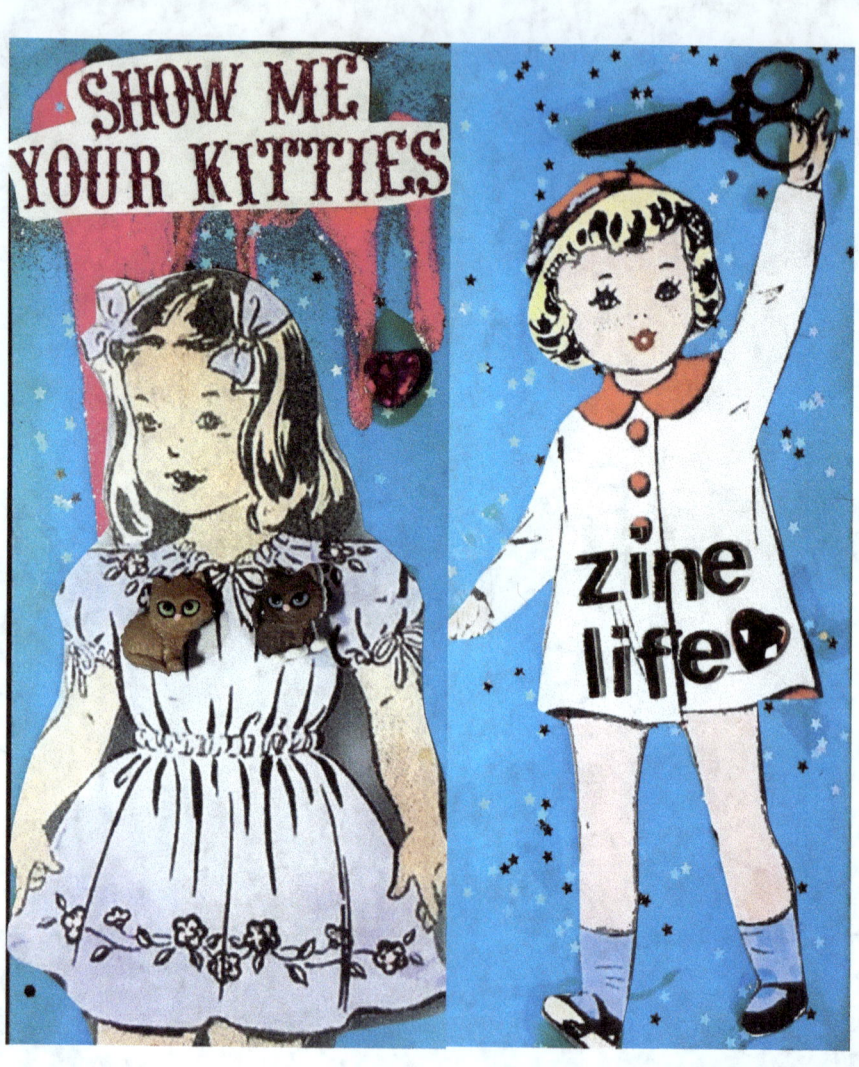

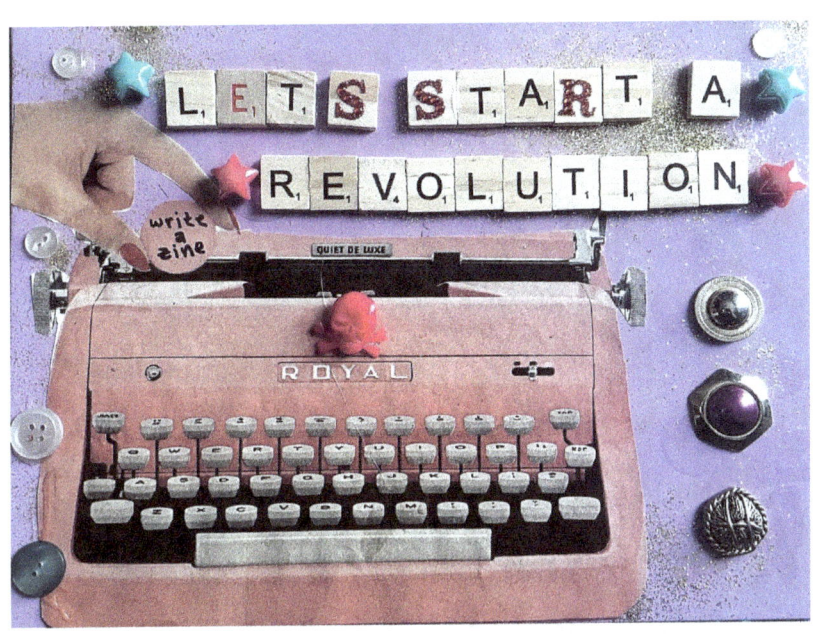

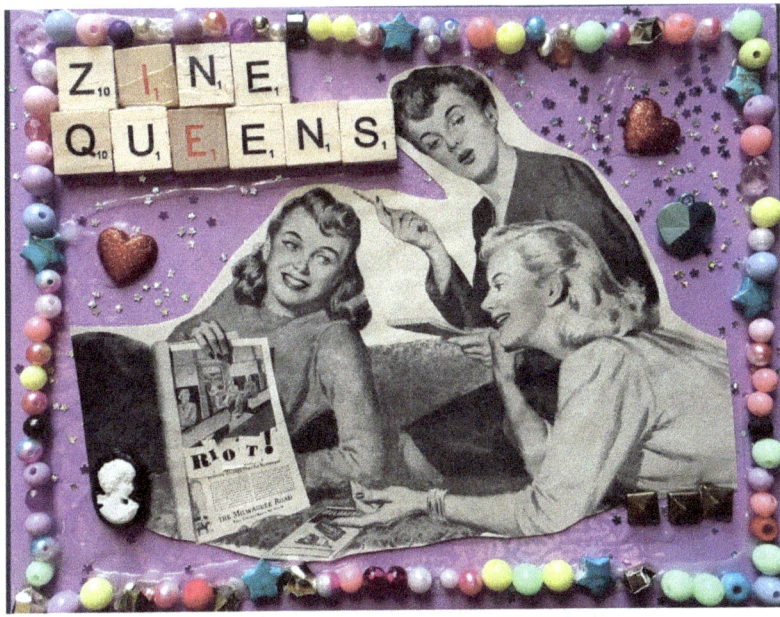

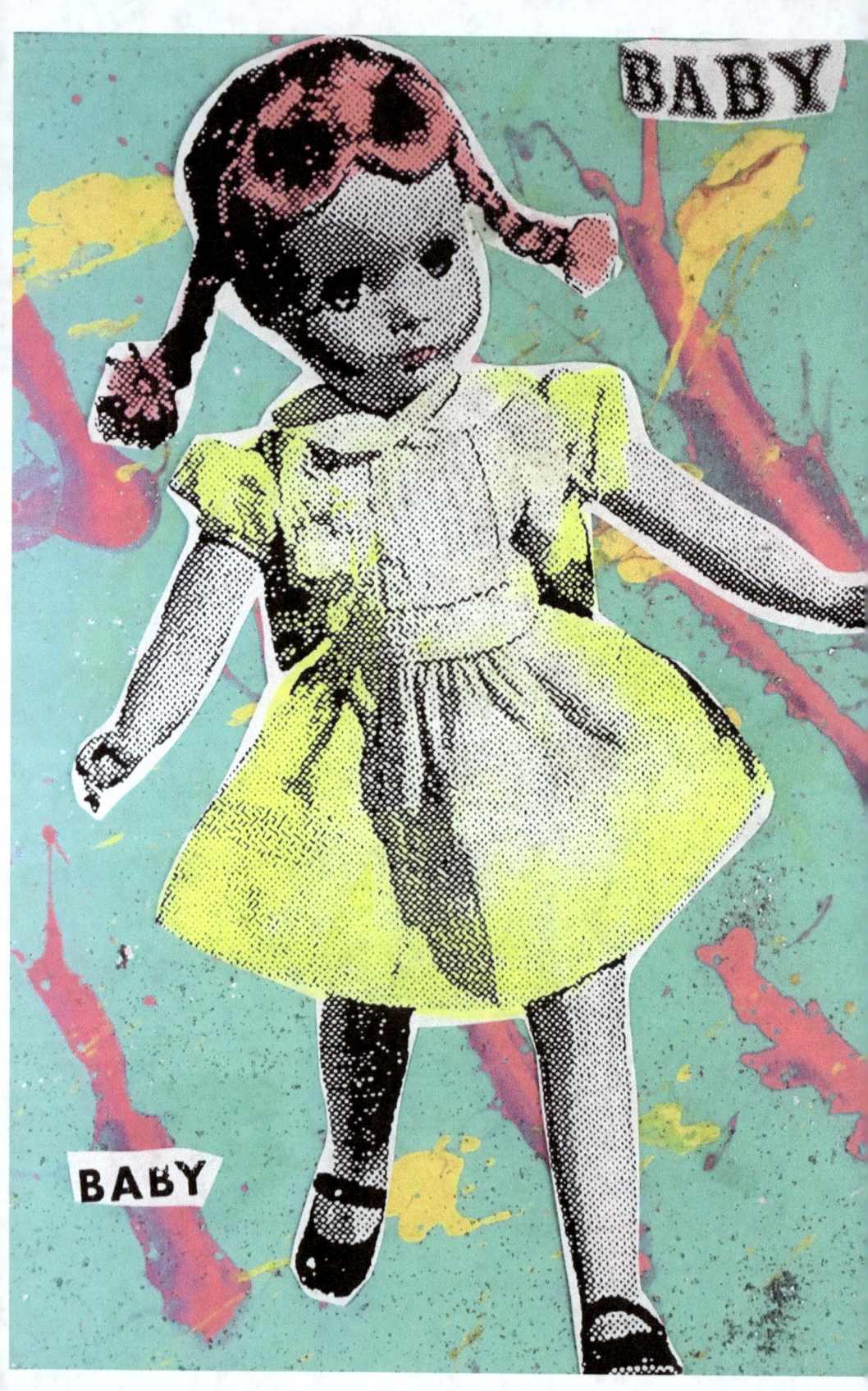

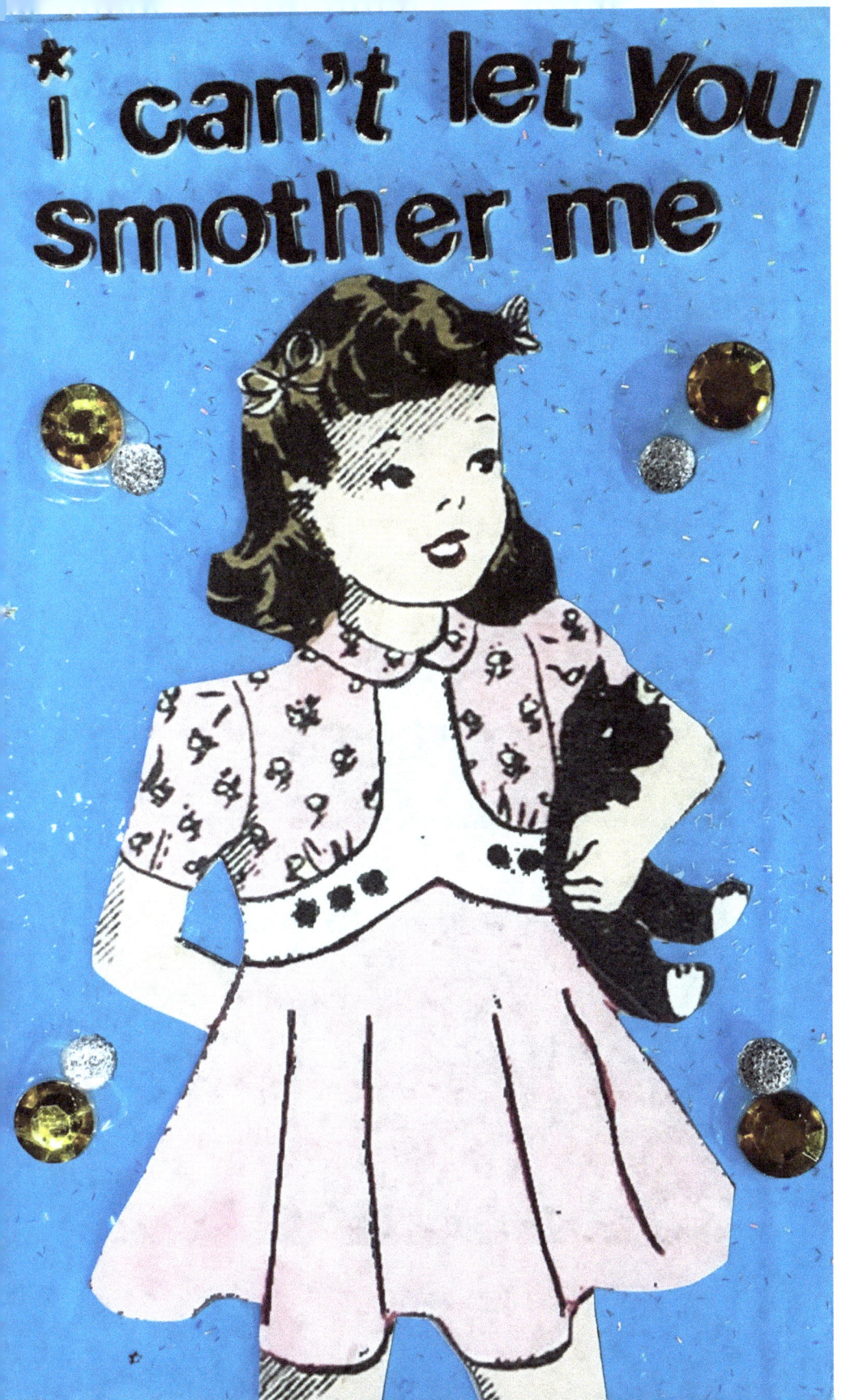

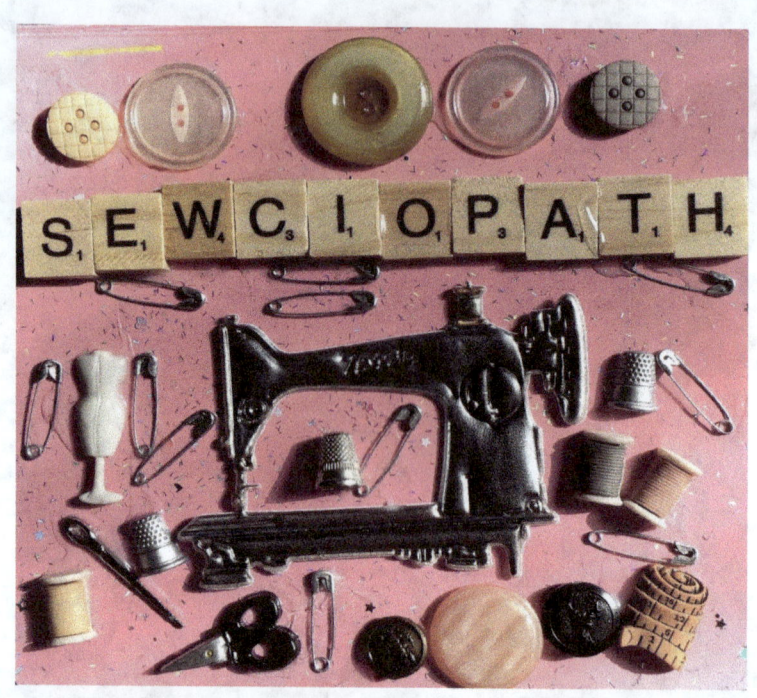

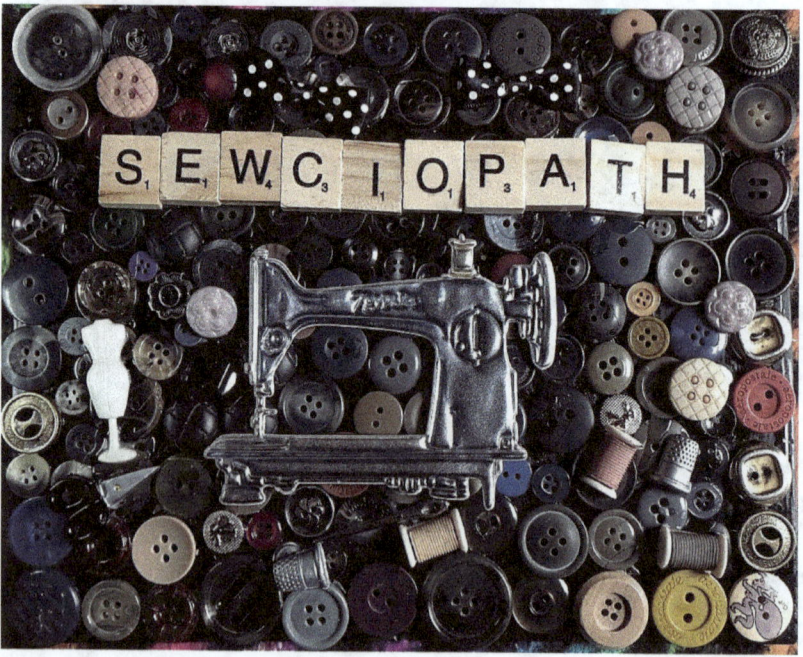

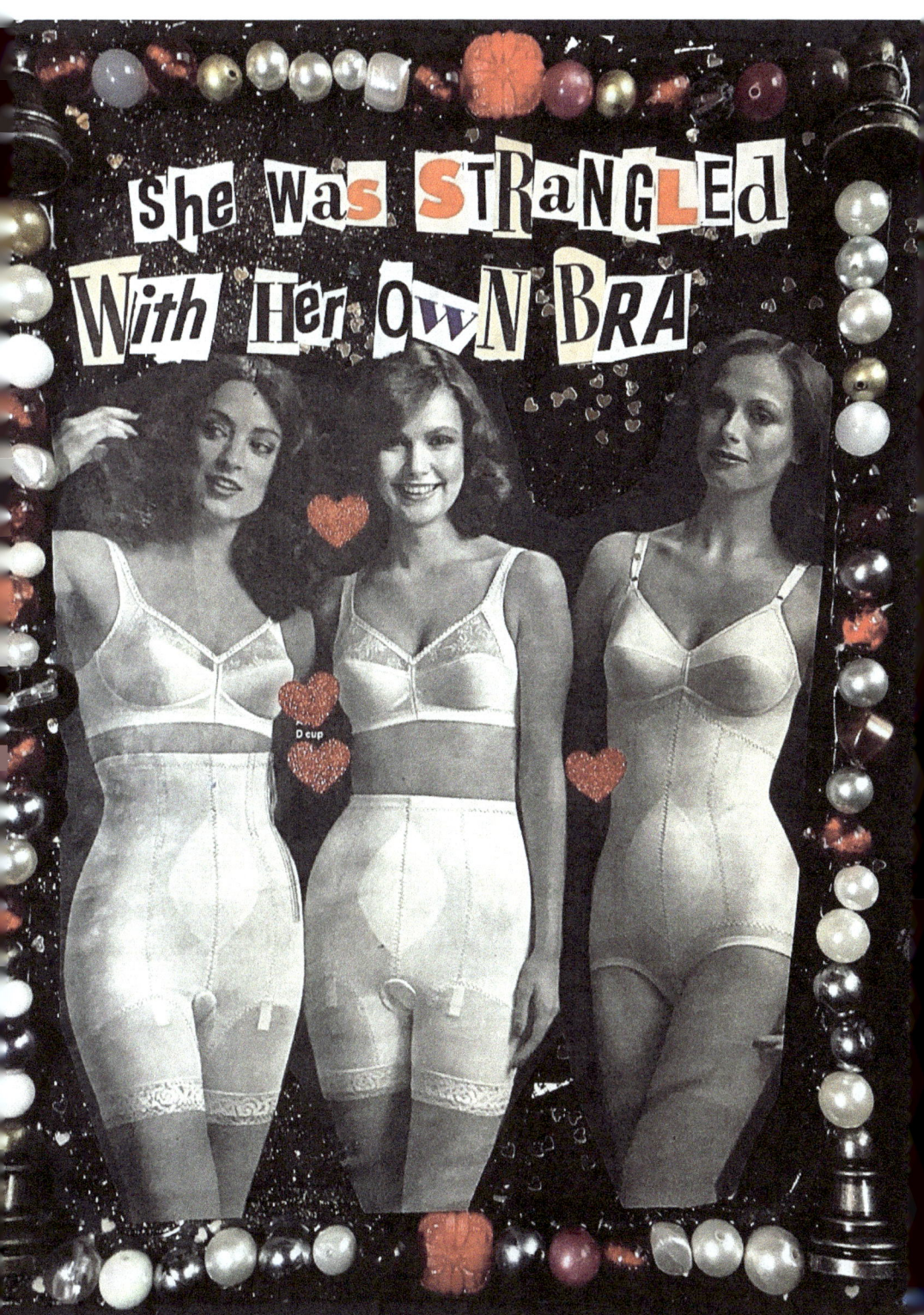

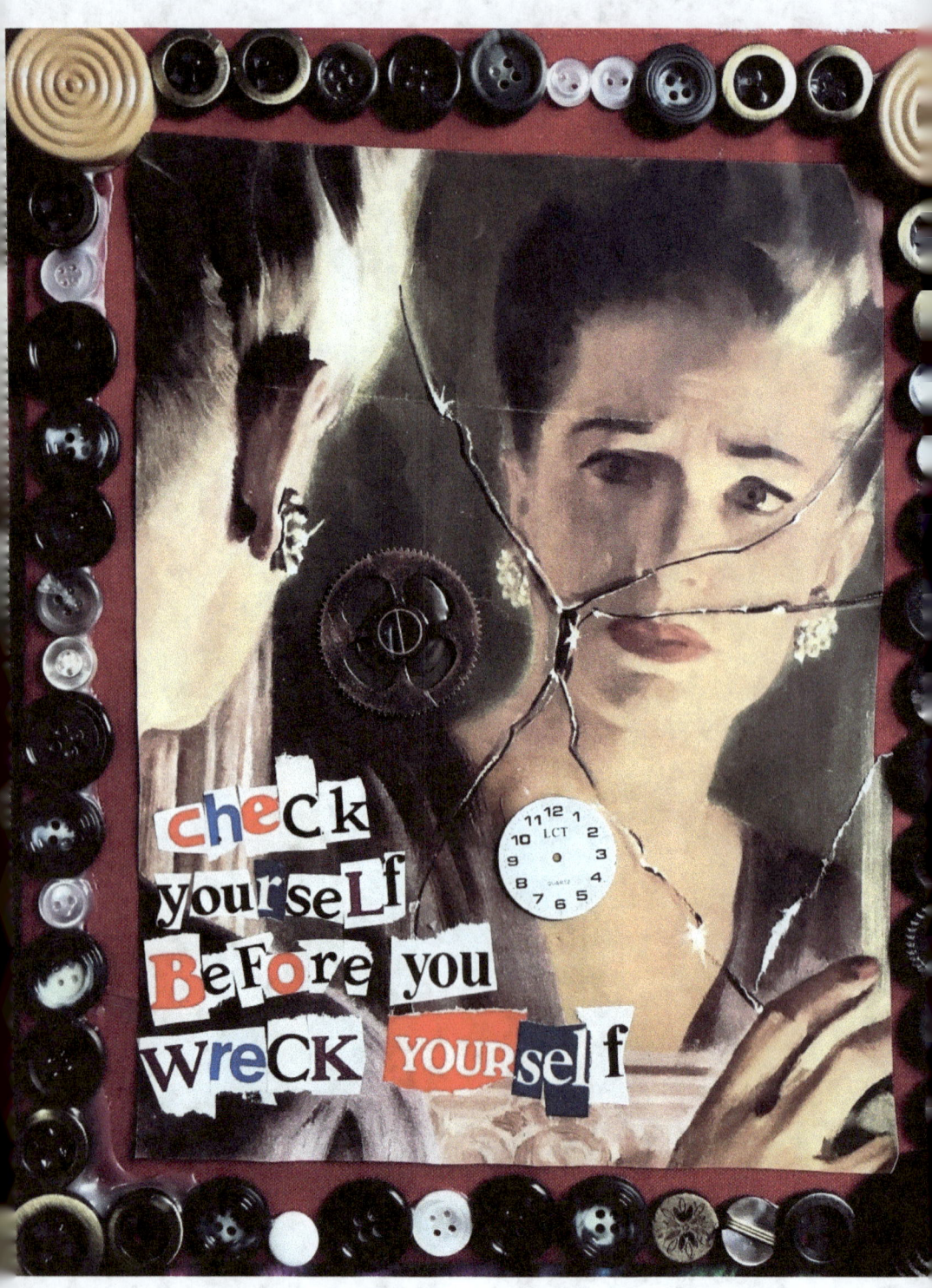

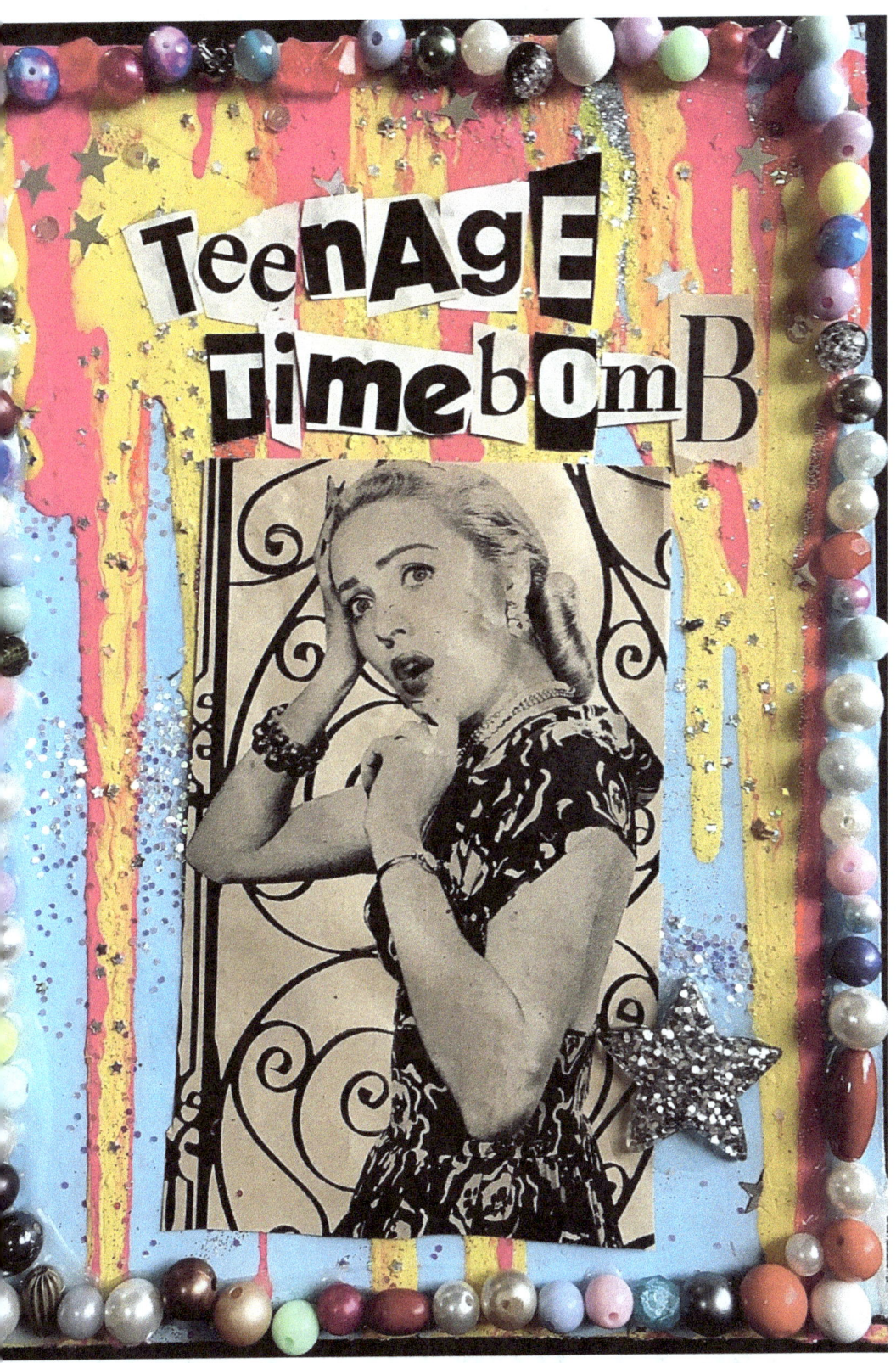

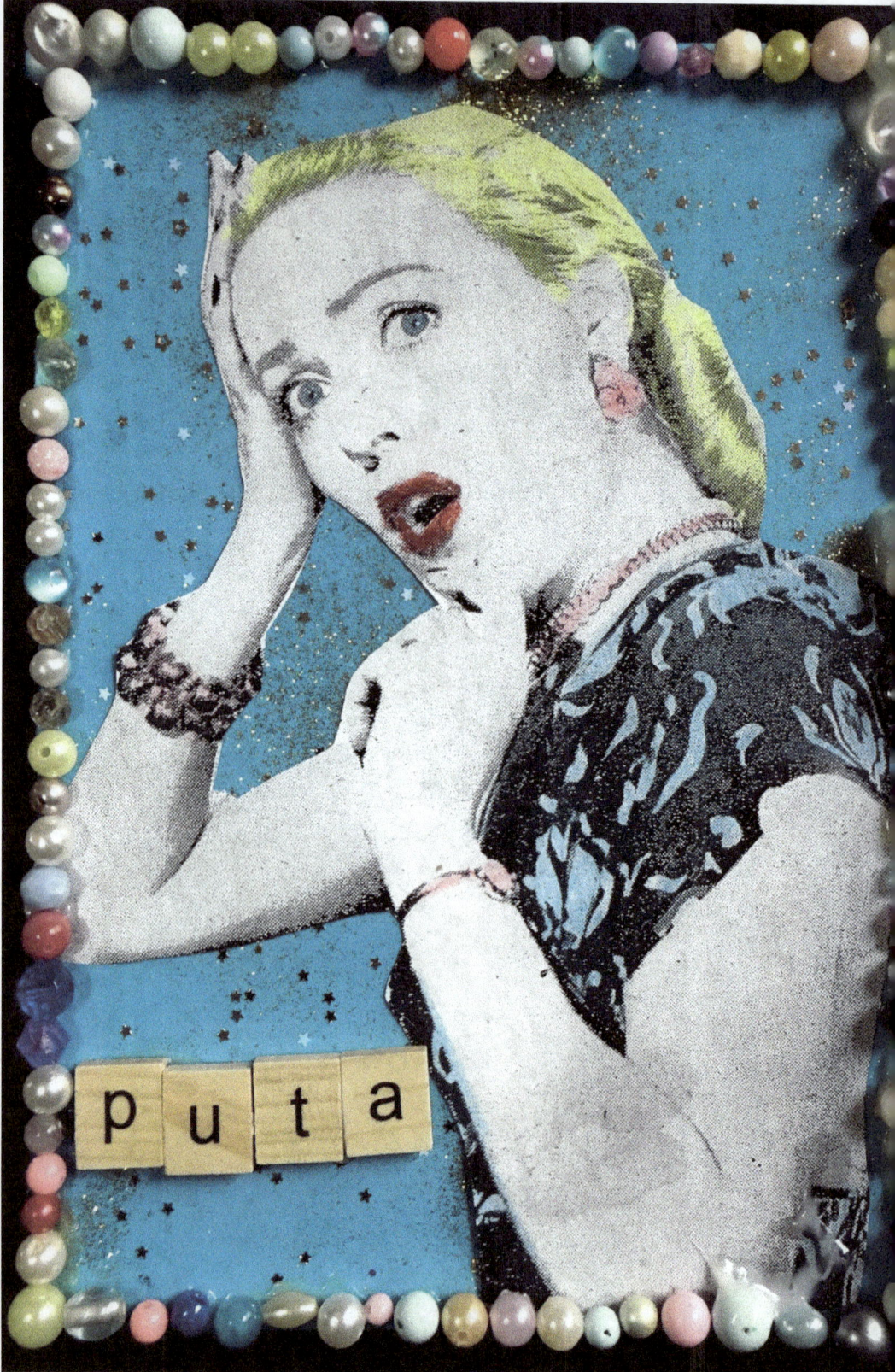

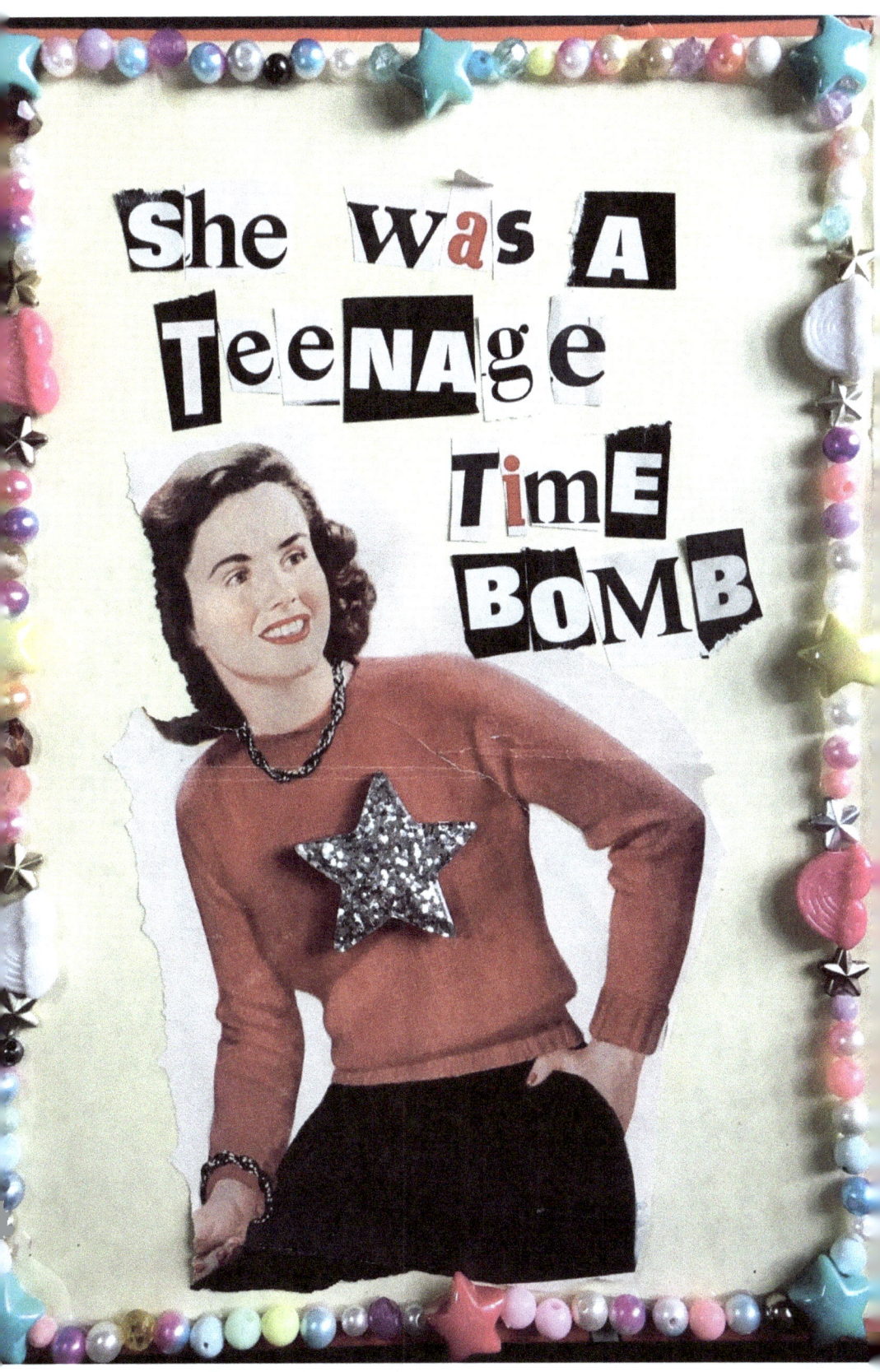

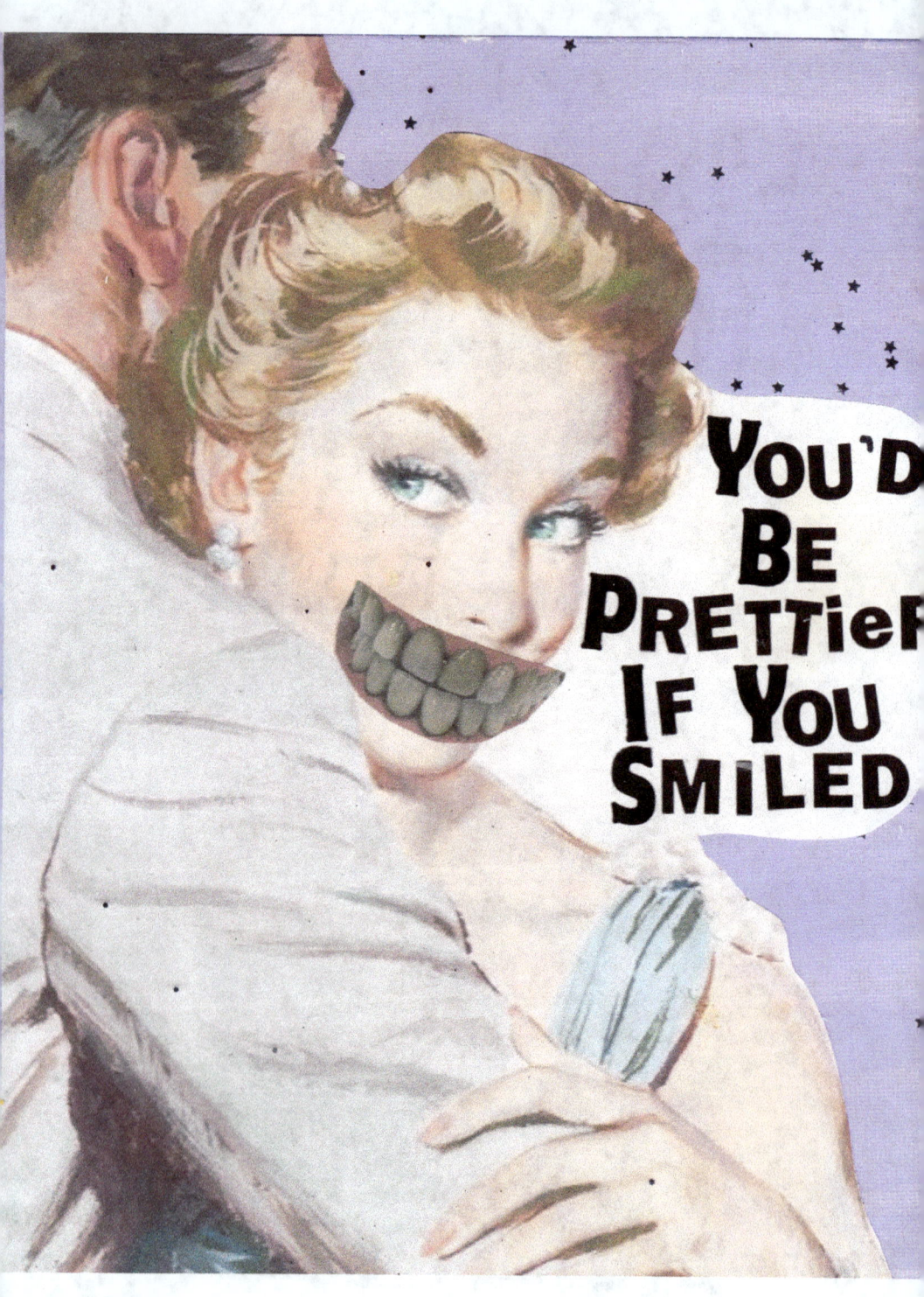

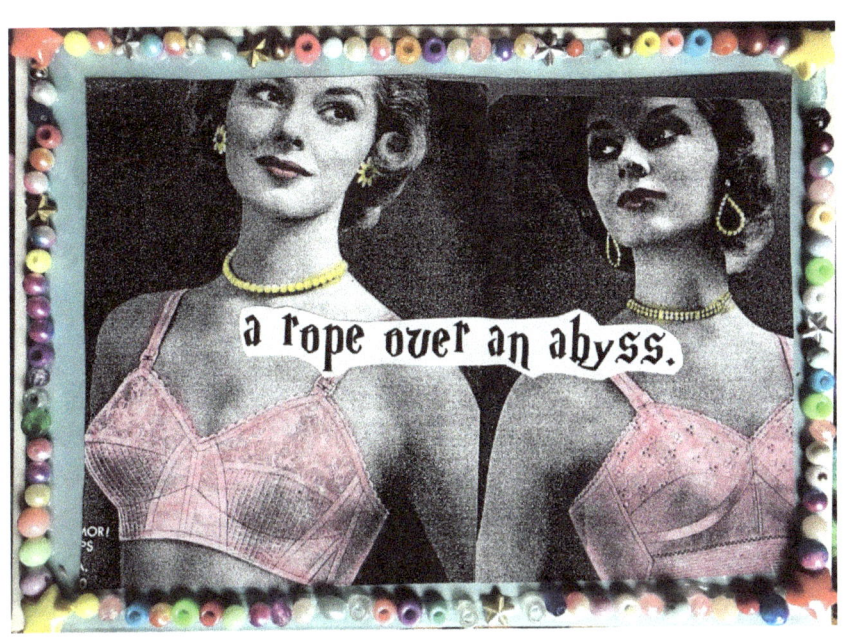

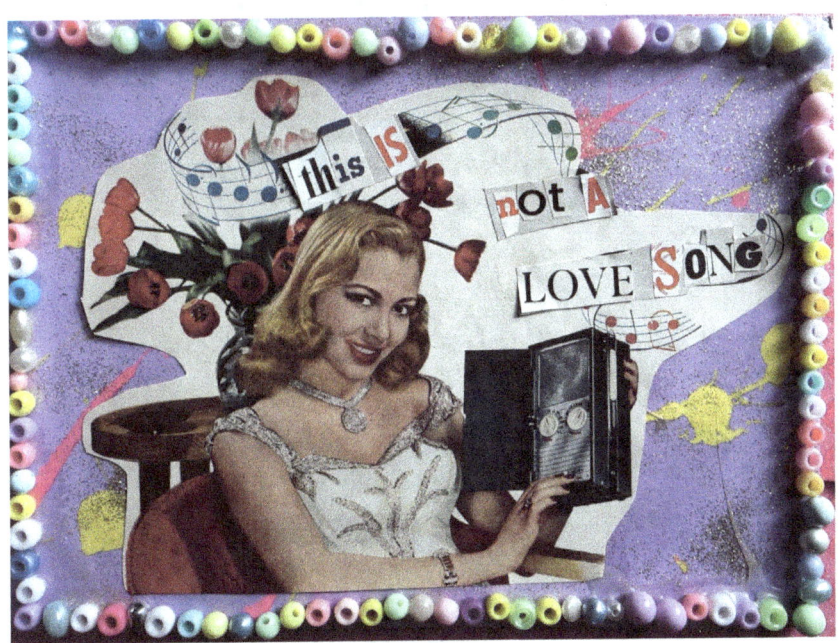

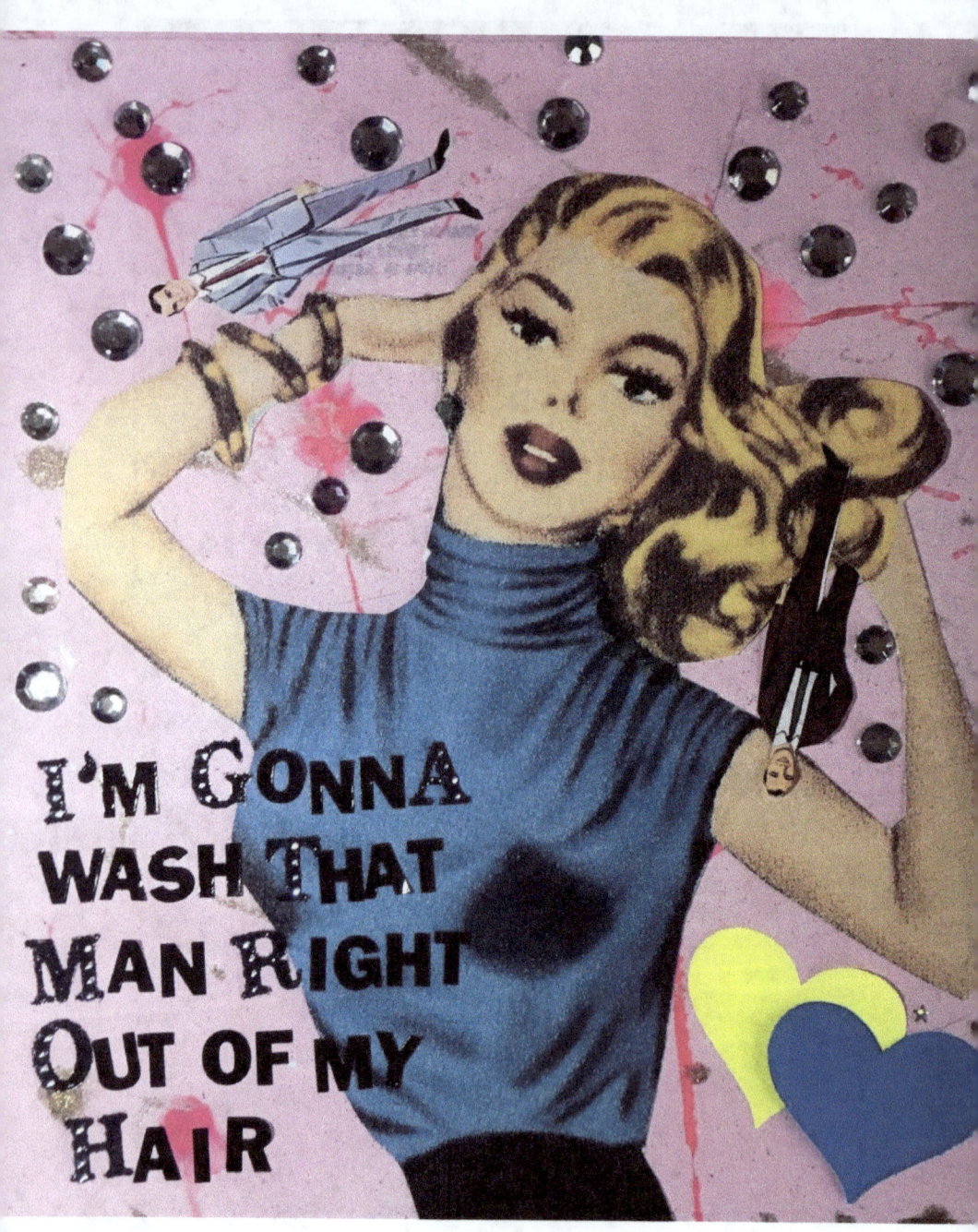

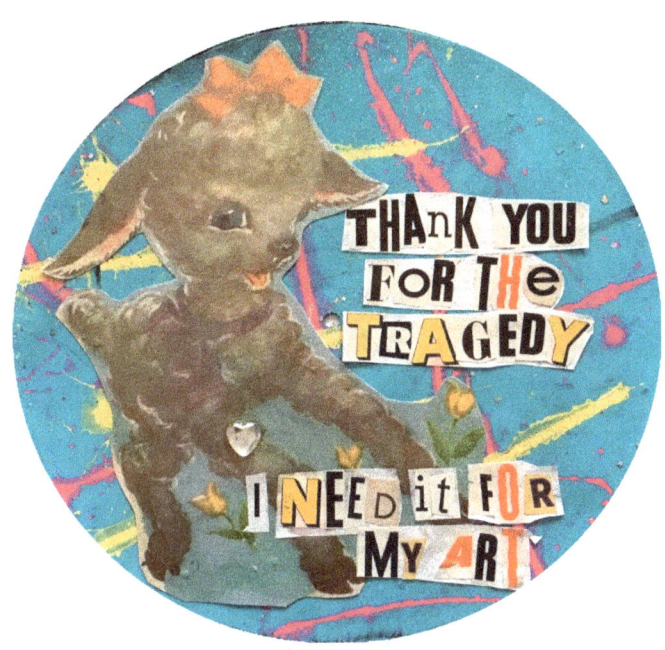

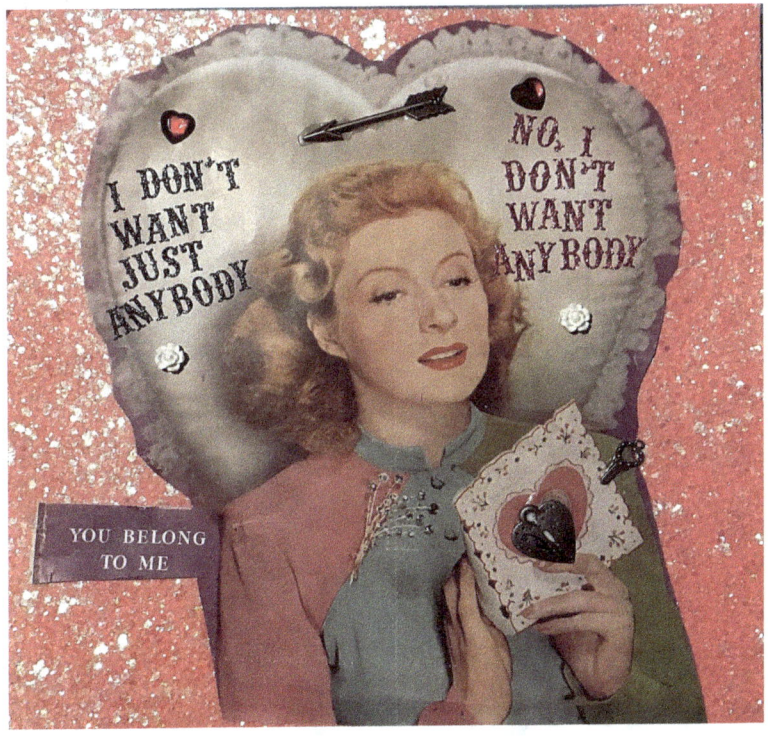

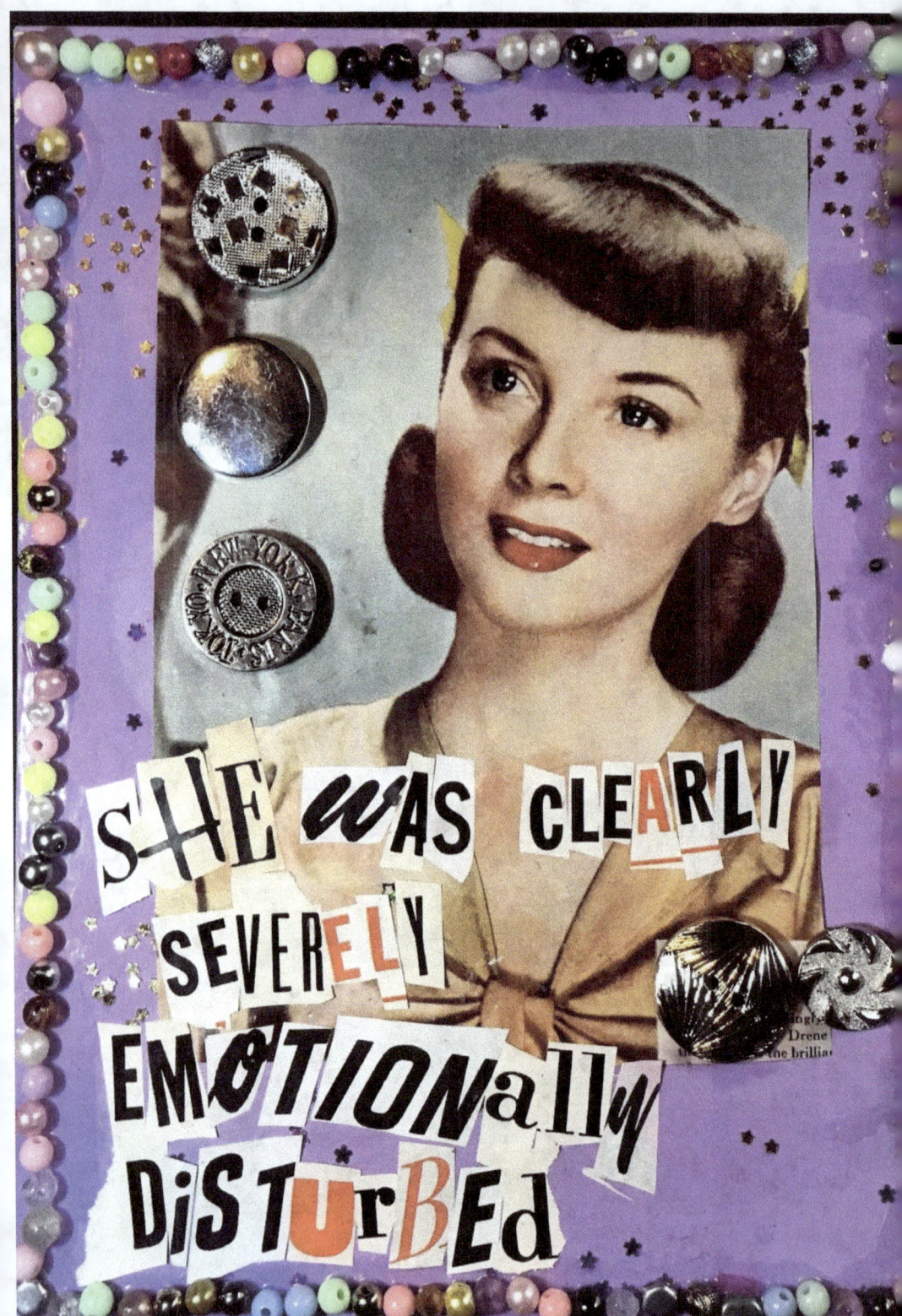

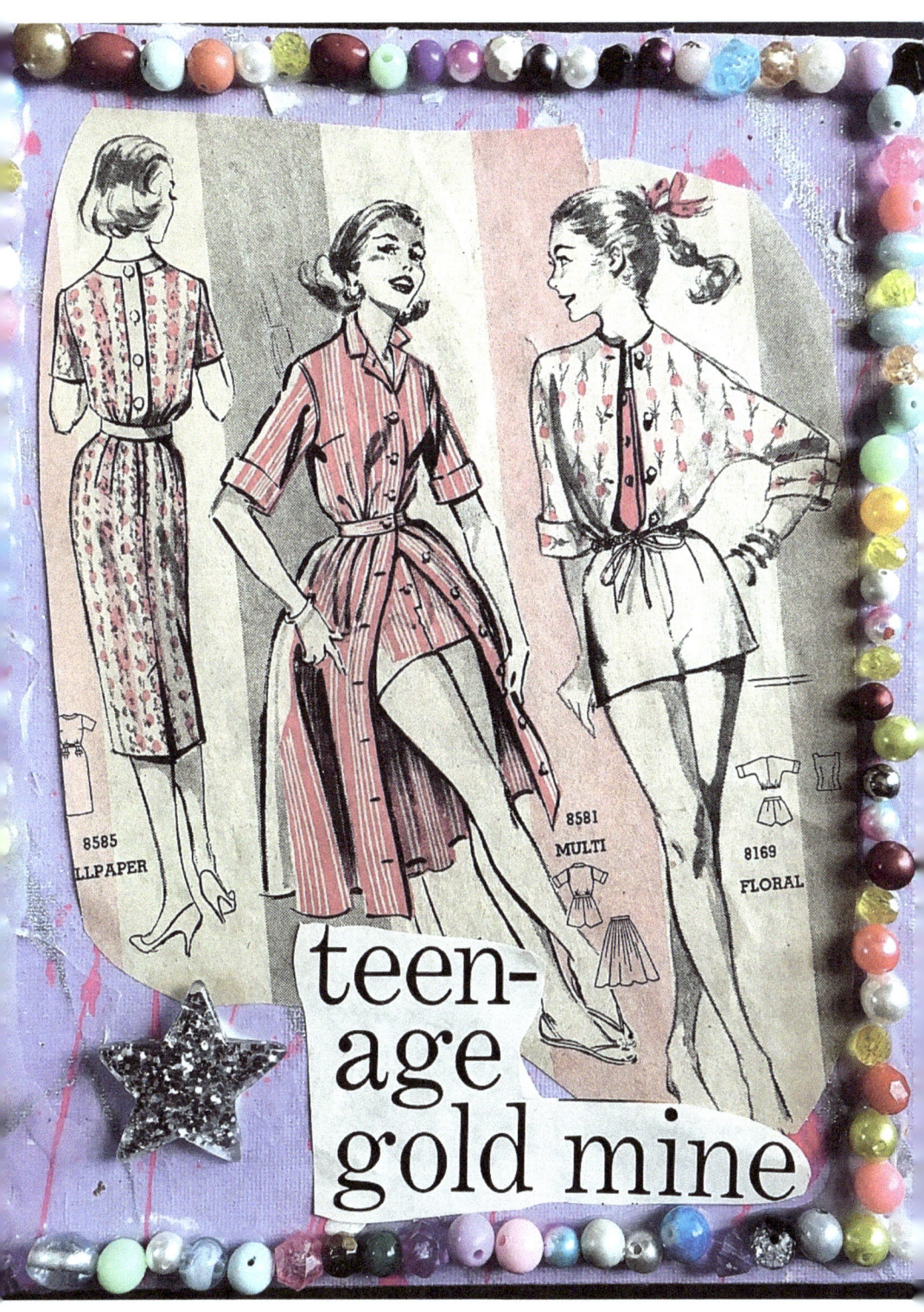

8585
LLPAPER

8581
MULTI

8169
FLORAL

teen-
age
gold mine

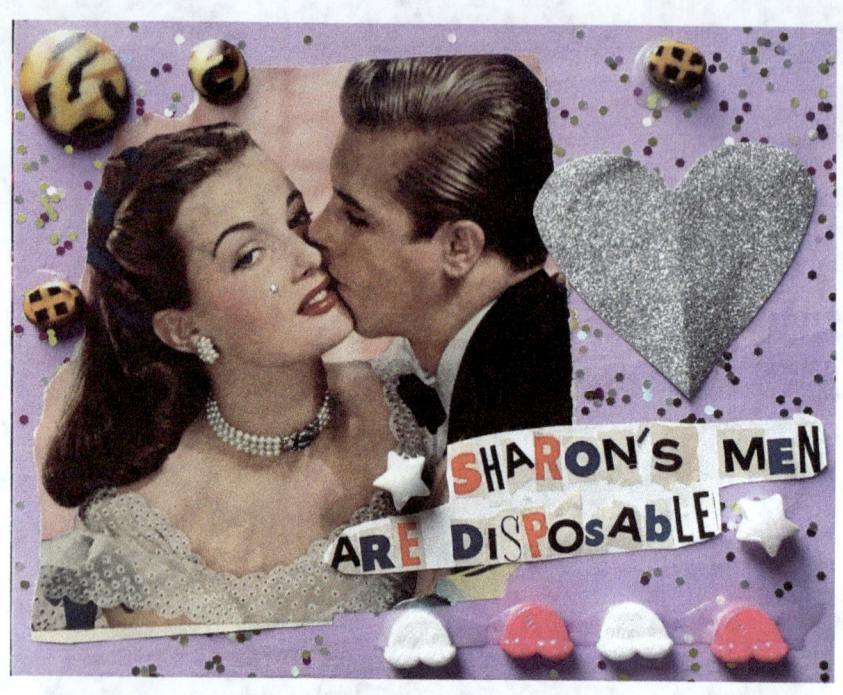

SHARON'S MEN ARE DISPOSABLE

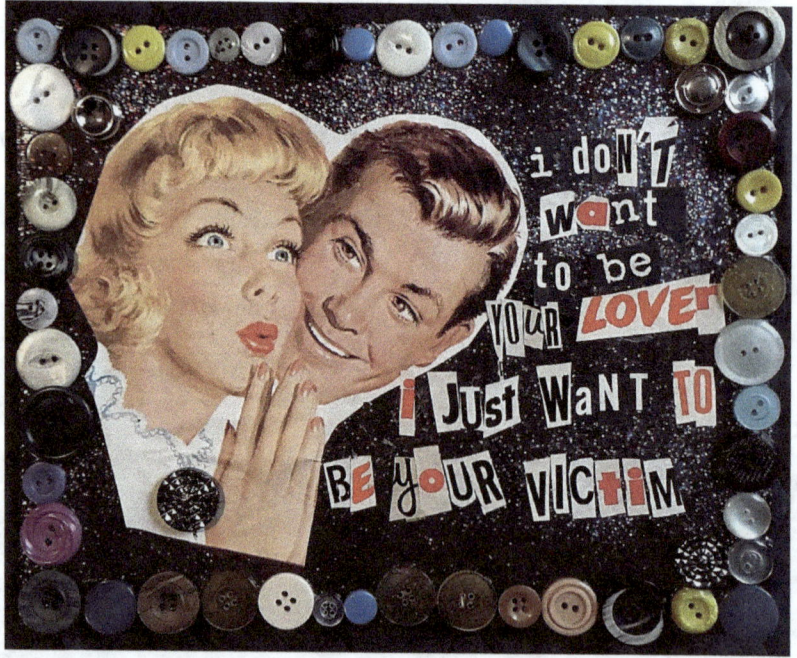

i don't want to be your LOVER i just want to be your VICTIM

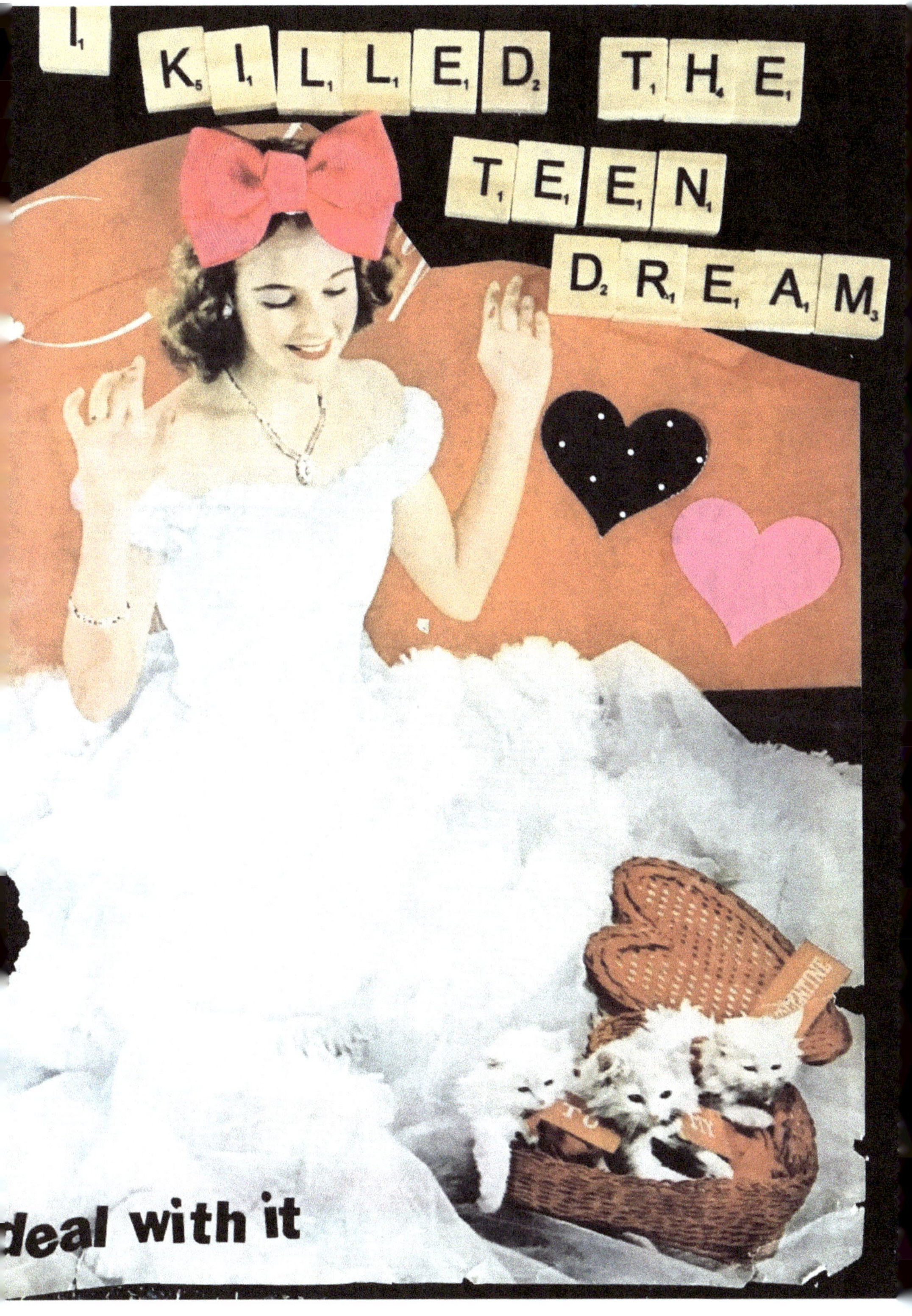
I KILLED THE
TEEN
DREAM
deal with it

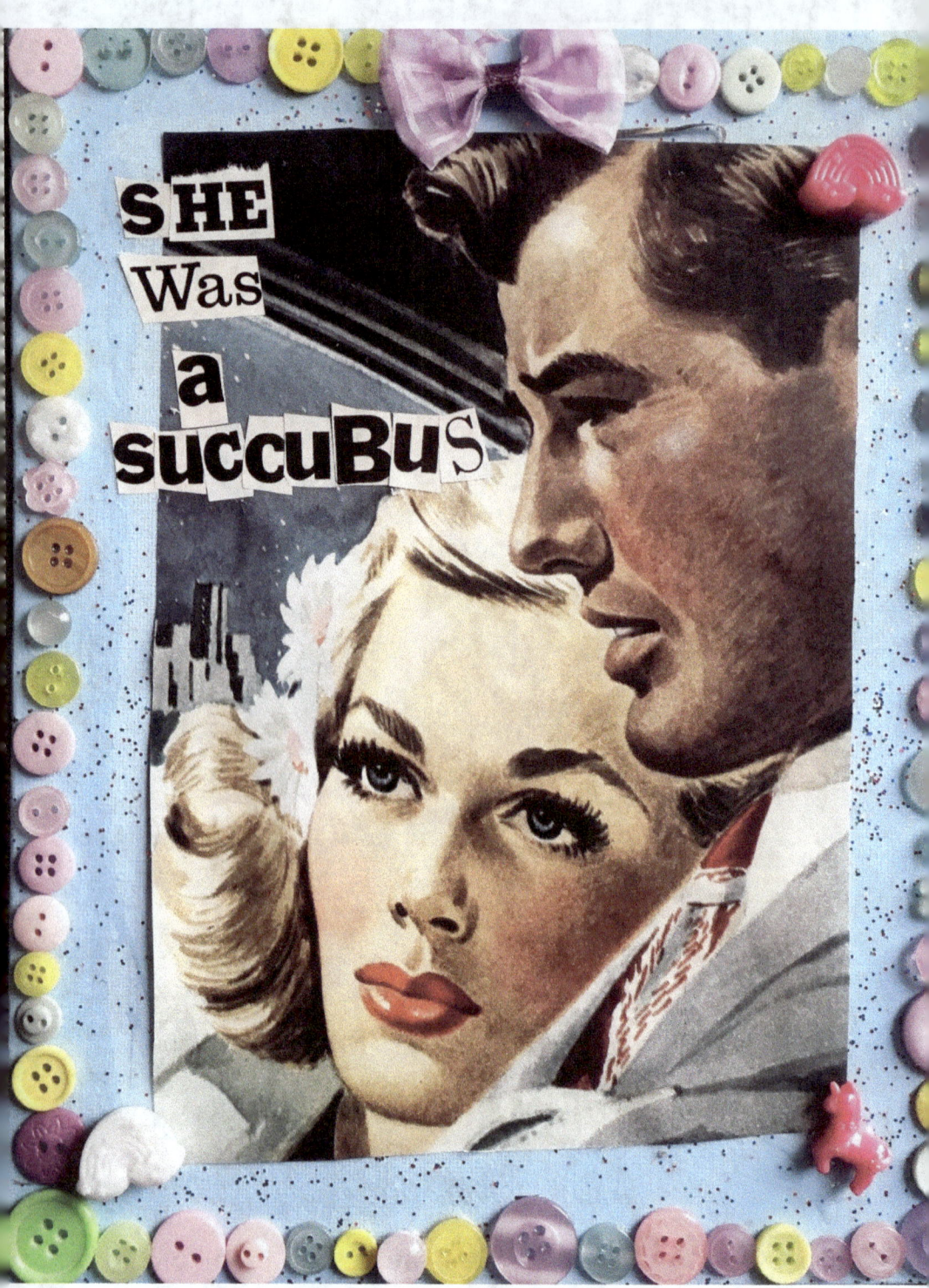

SHE Was a succuBus

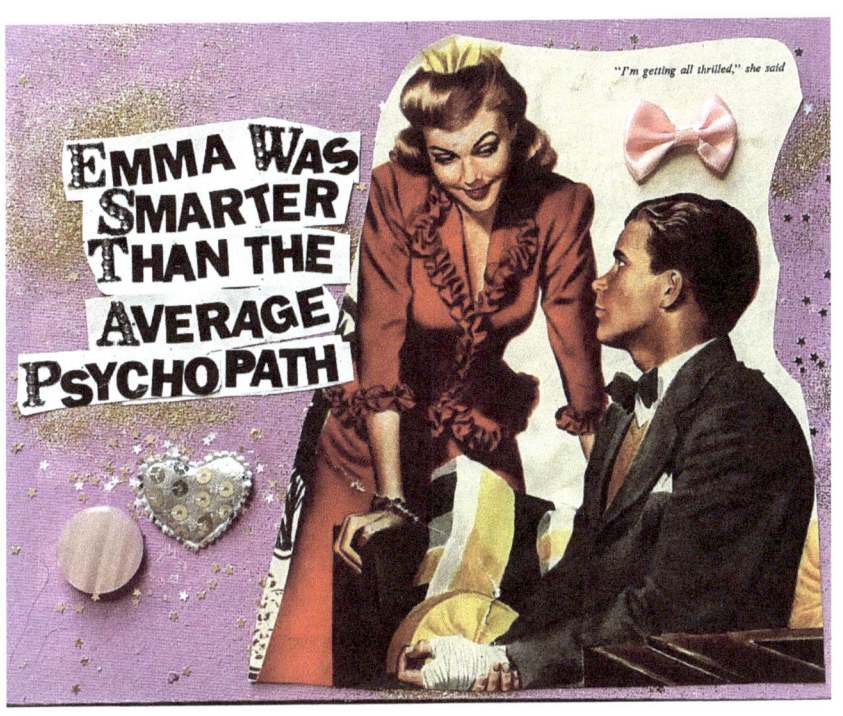

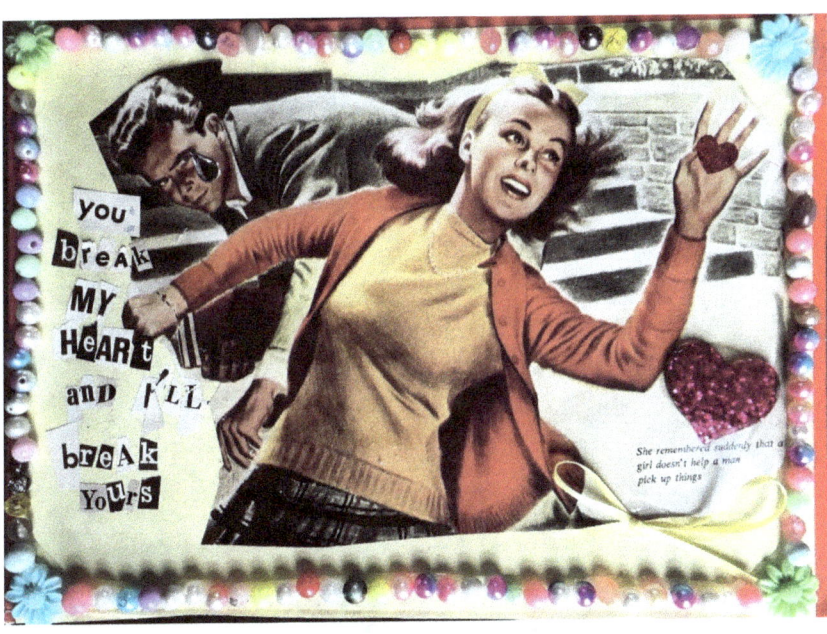

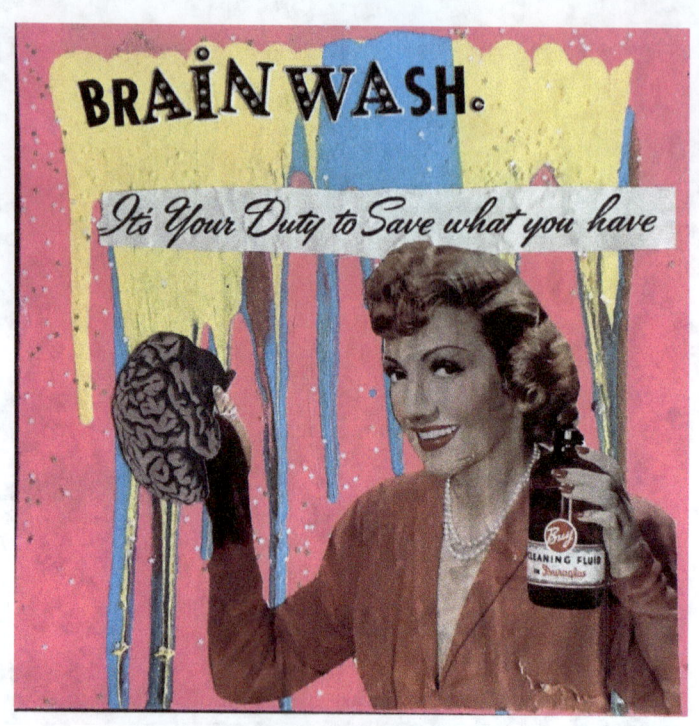

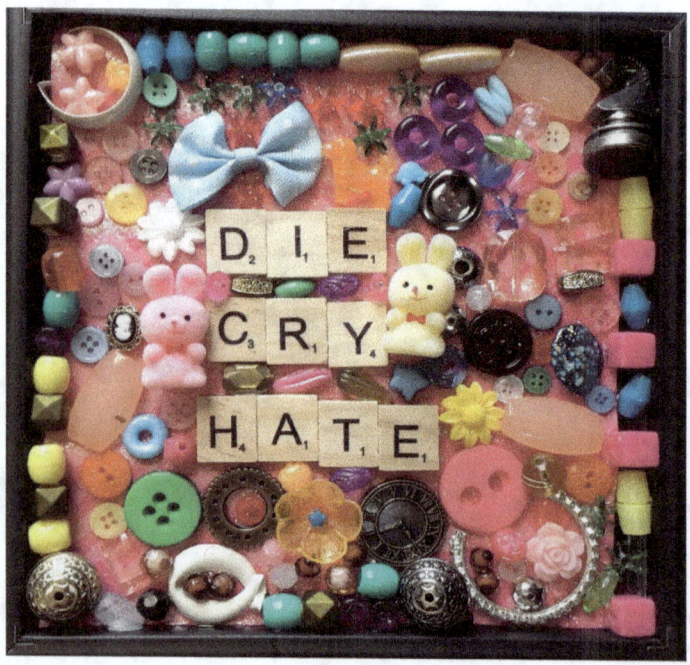

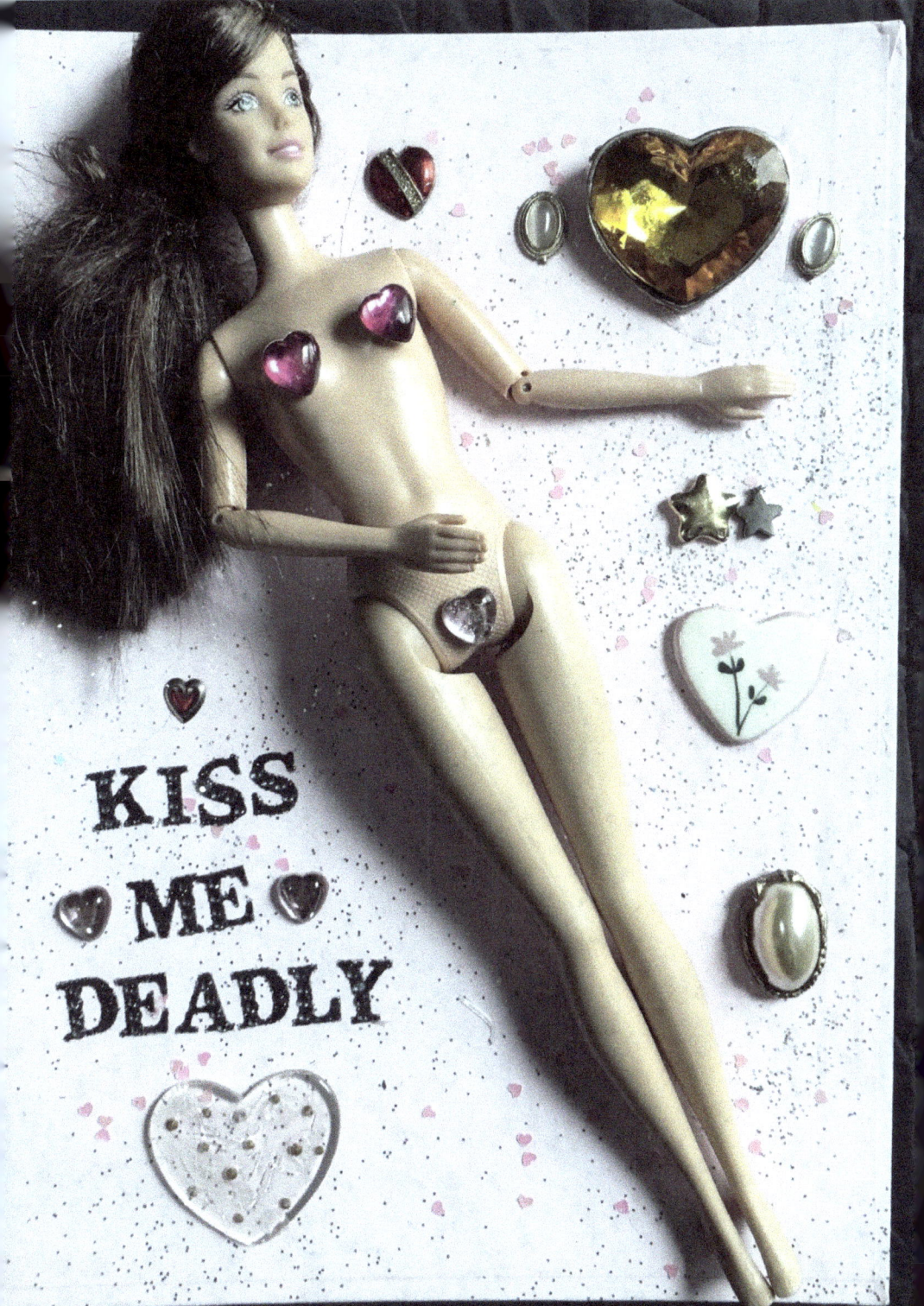

KISS
ME
DEADLY

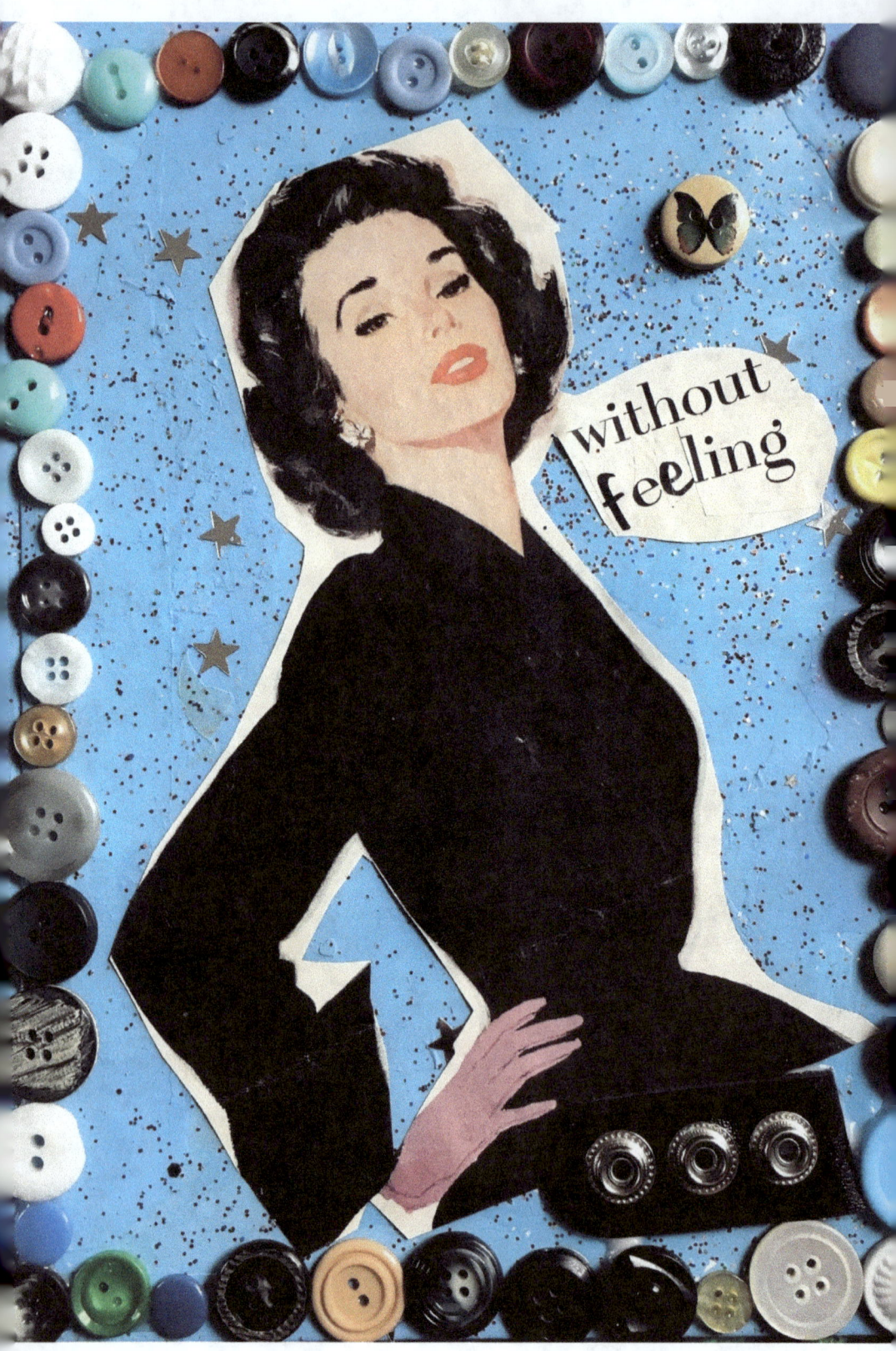

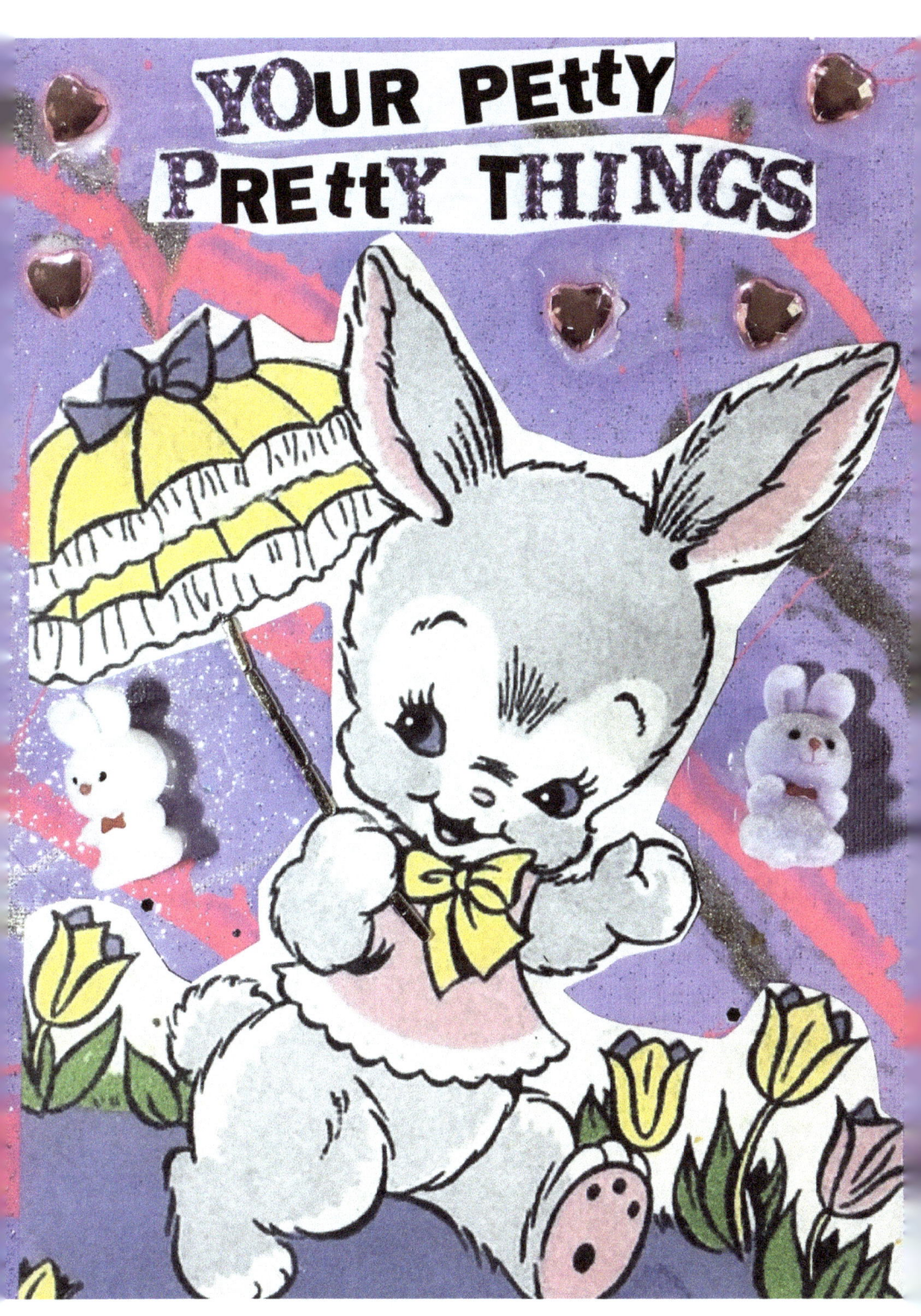

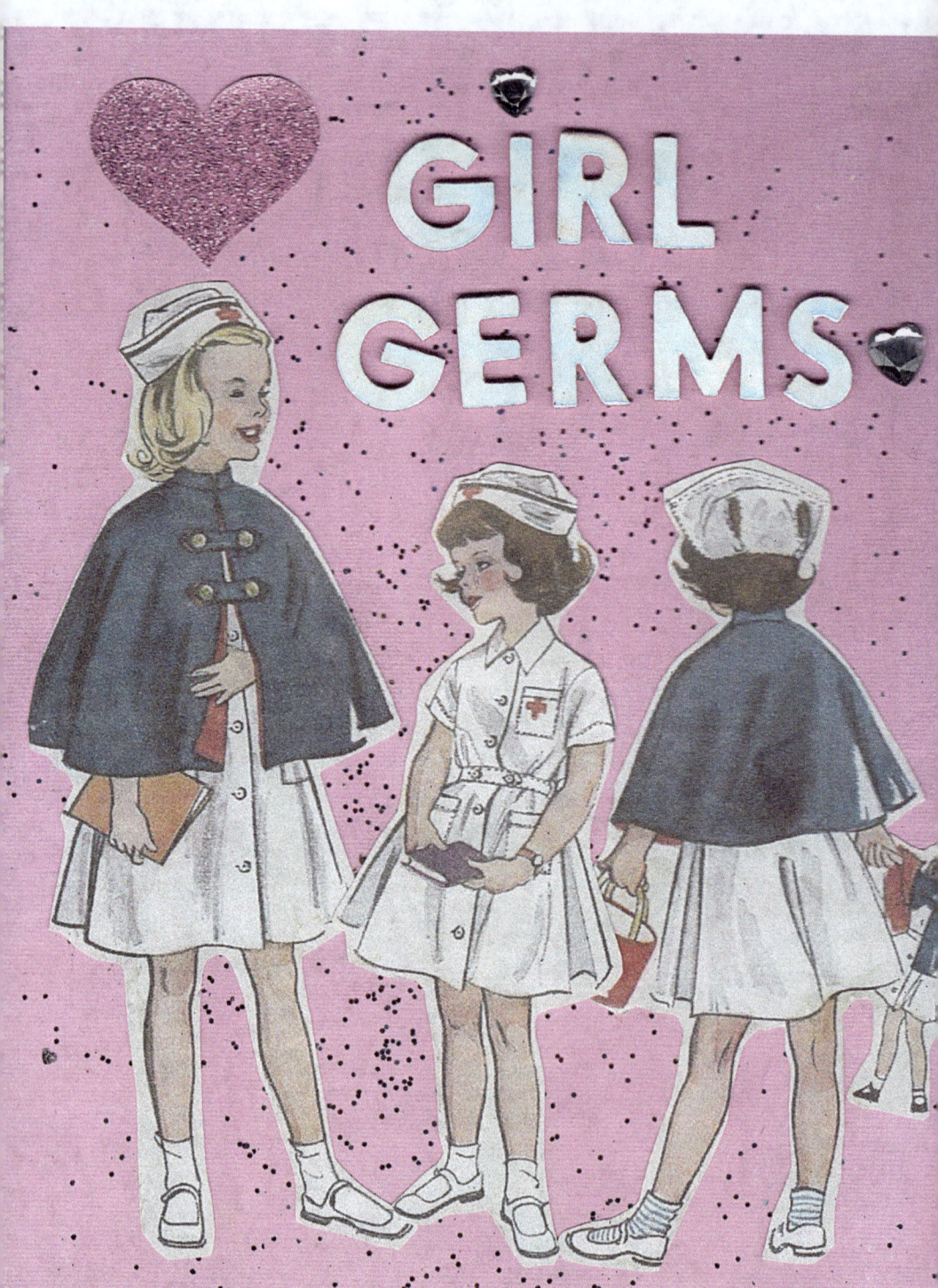

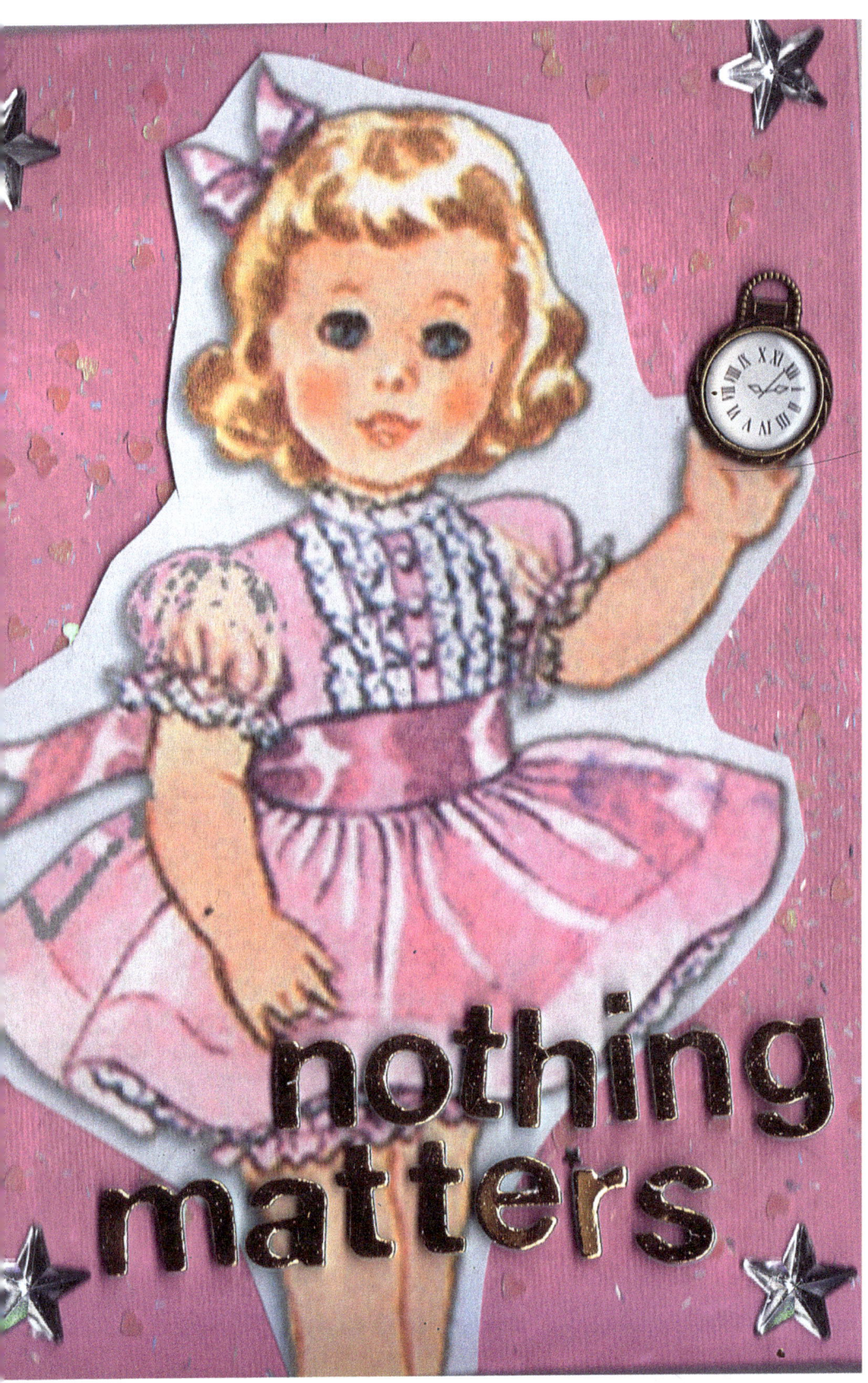

nothing matters

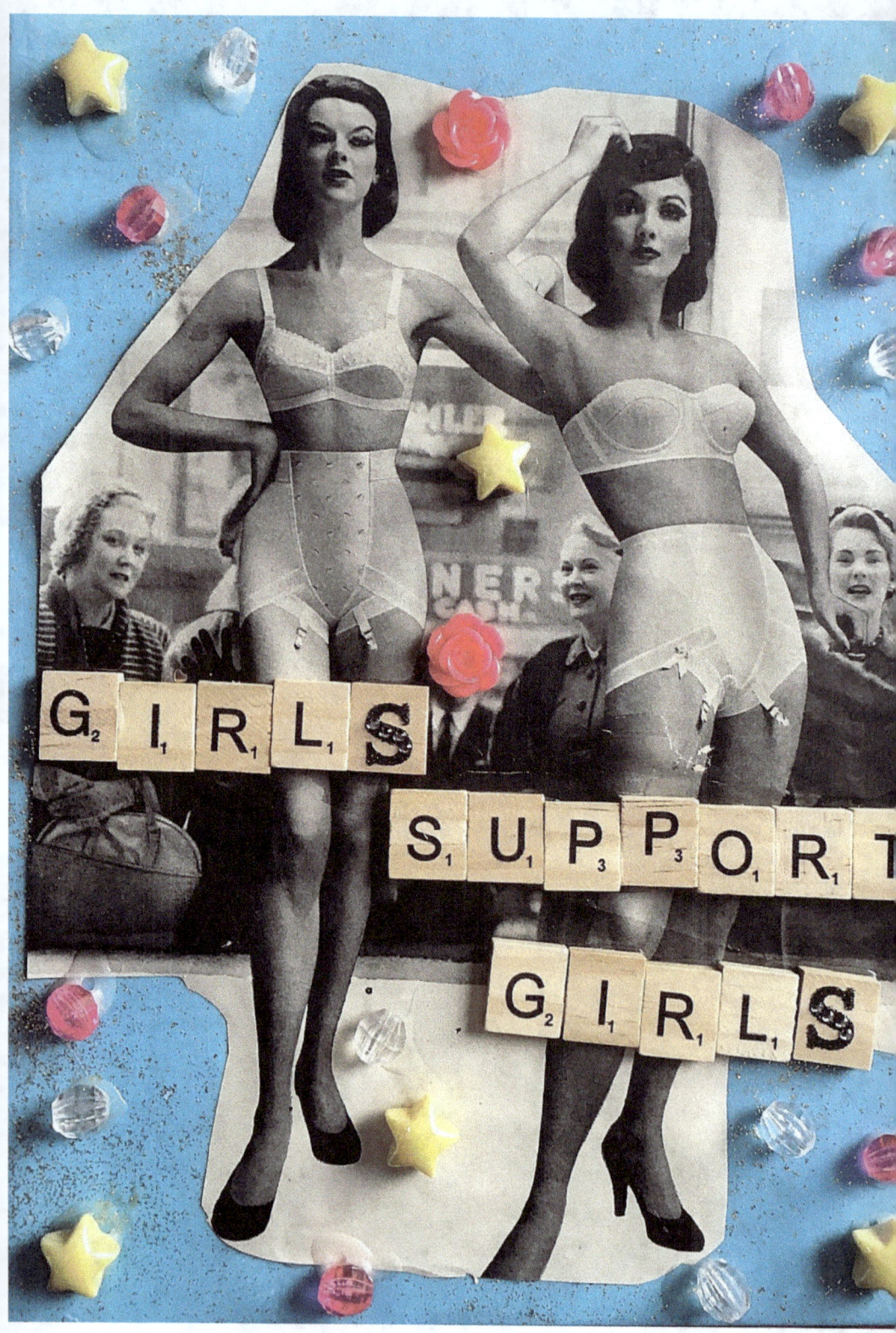

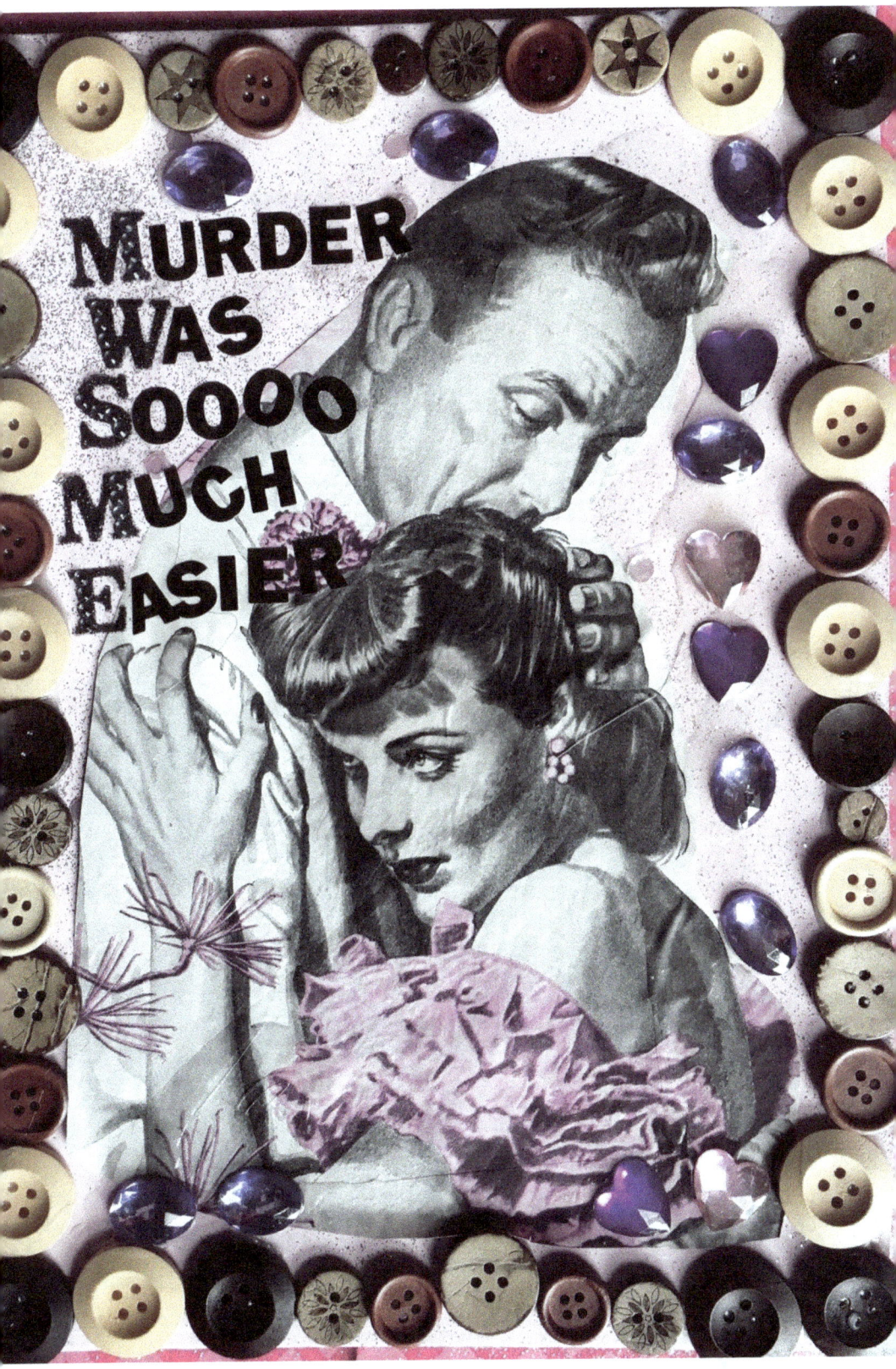

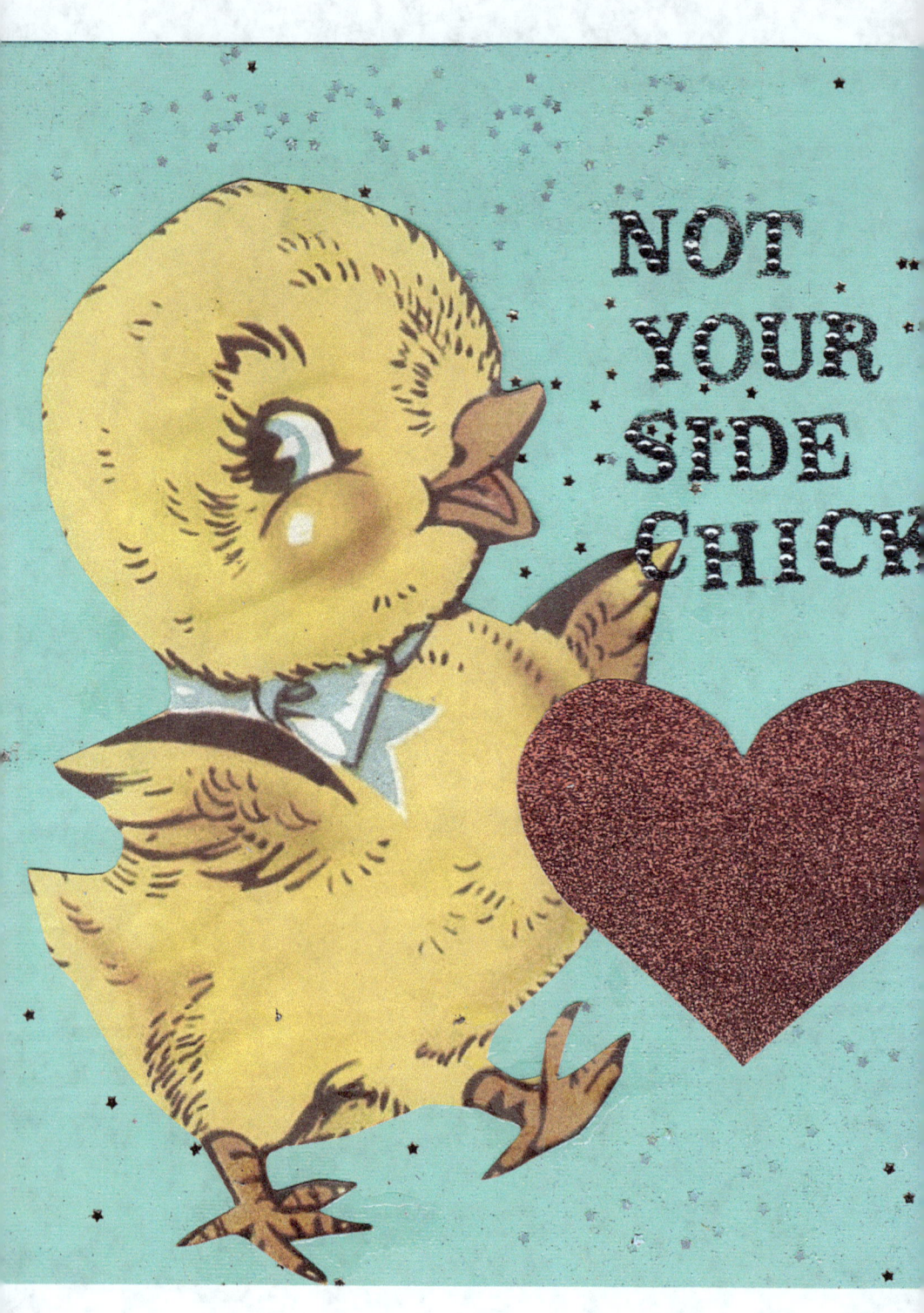

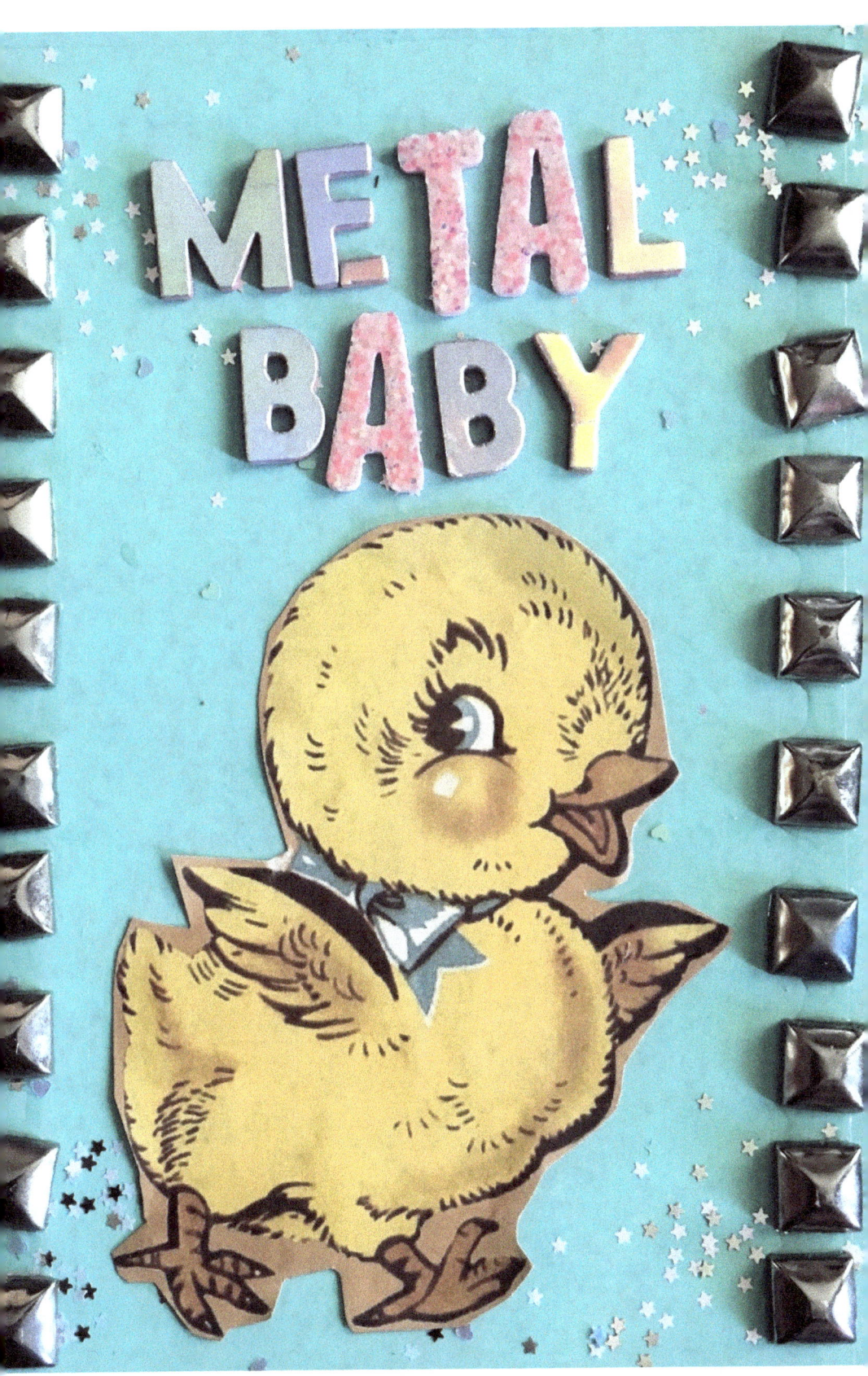

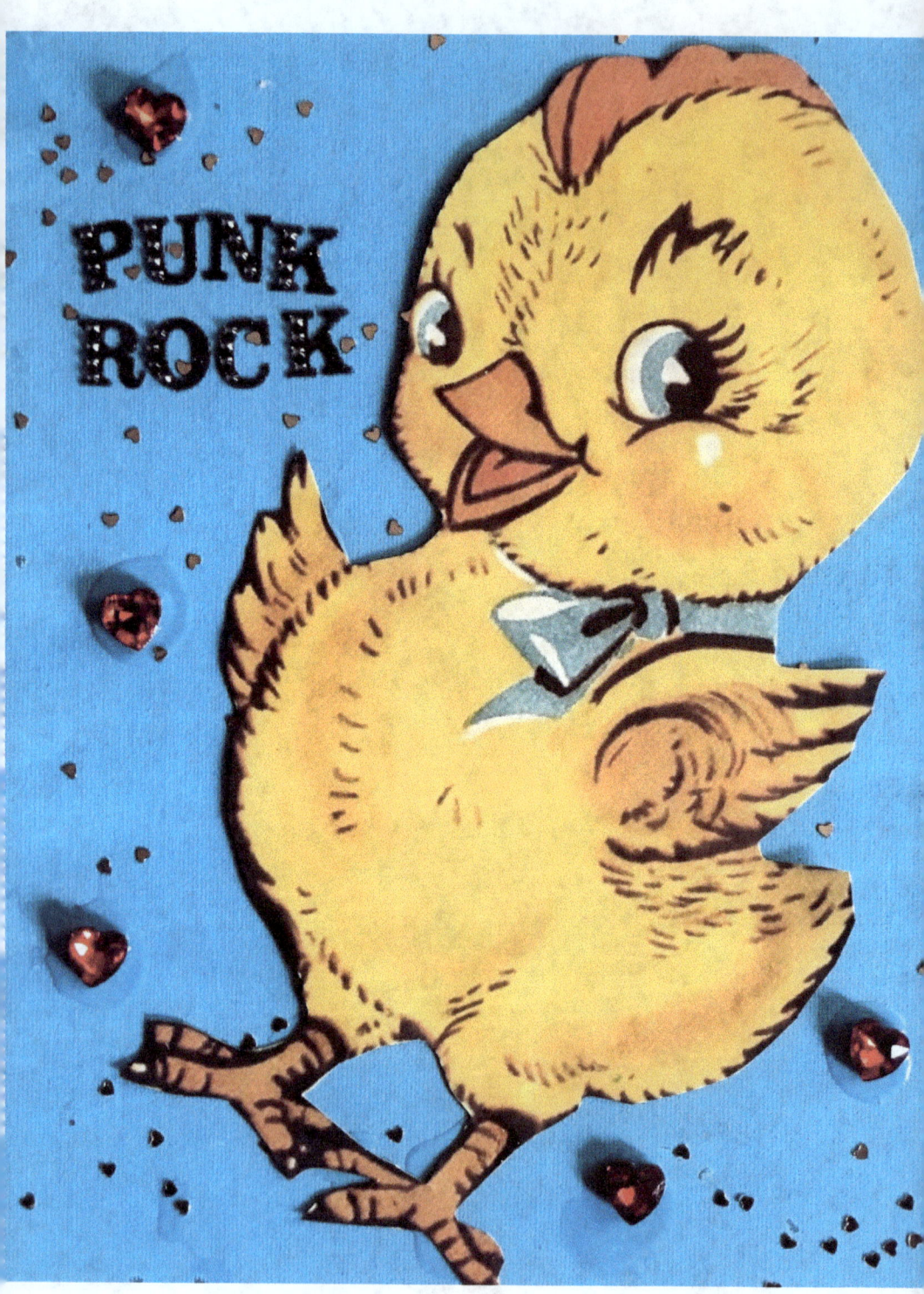

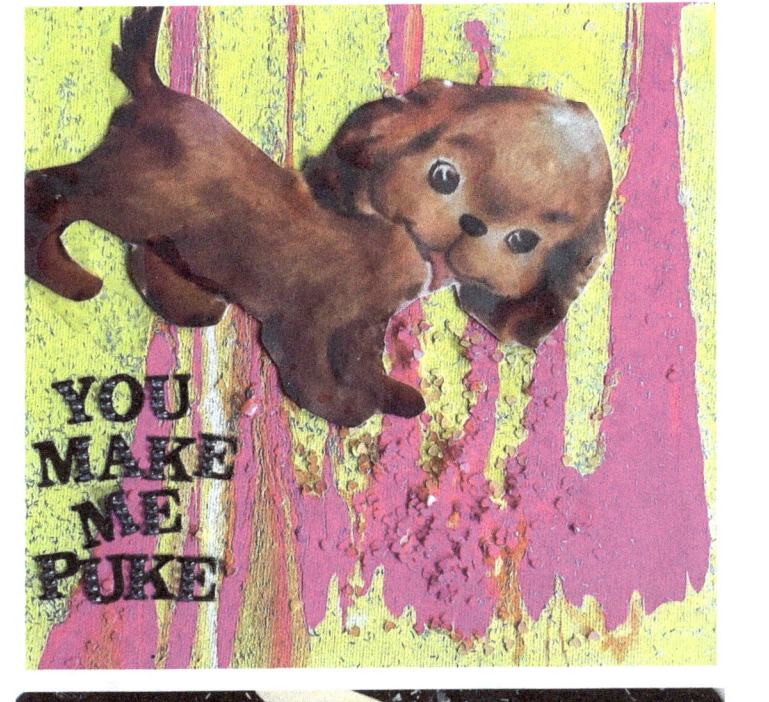

YOU MAKE ME PUKE

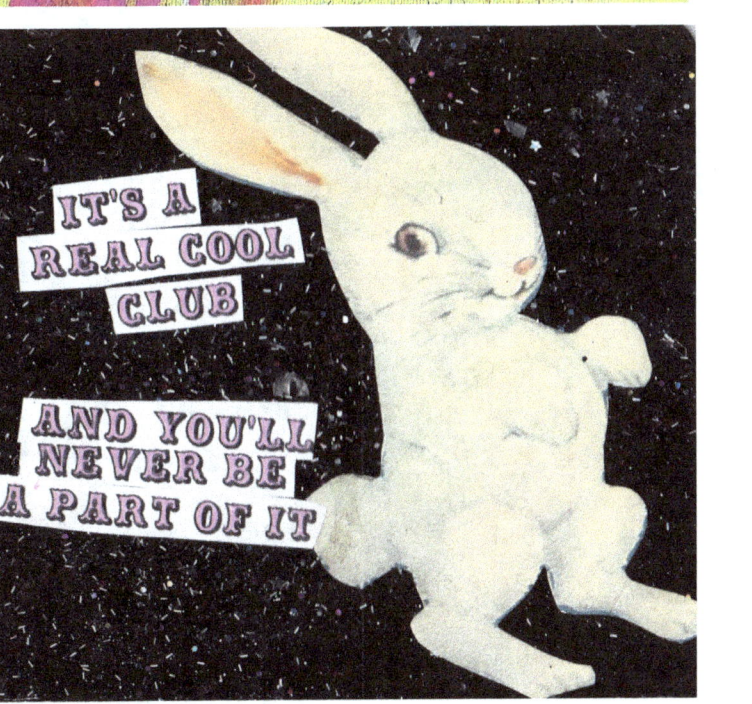

IT'S A REAL COOL CLUB

AND YOU'LL NEVER BE A PART OF IT

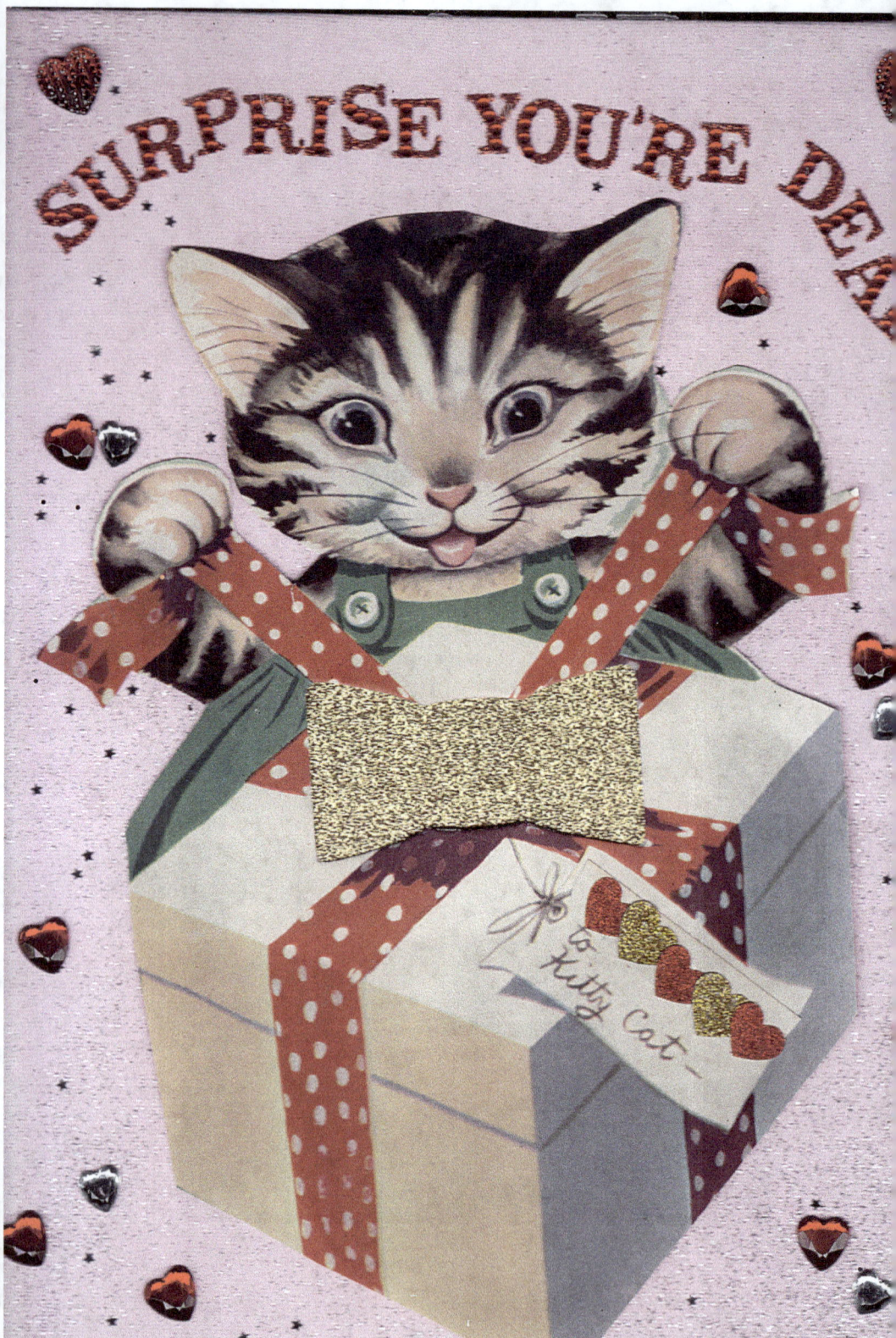

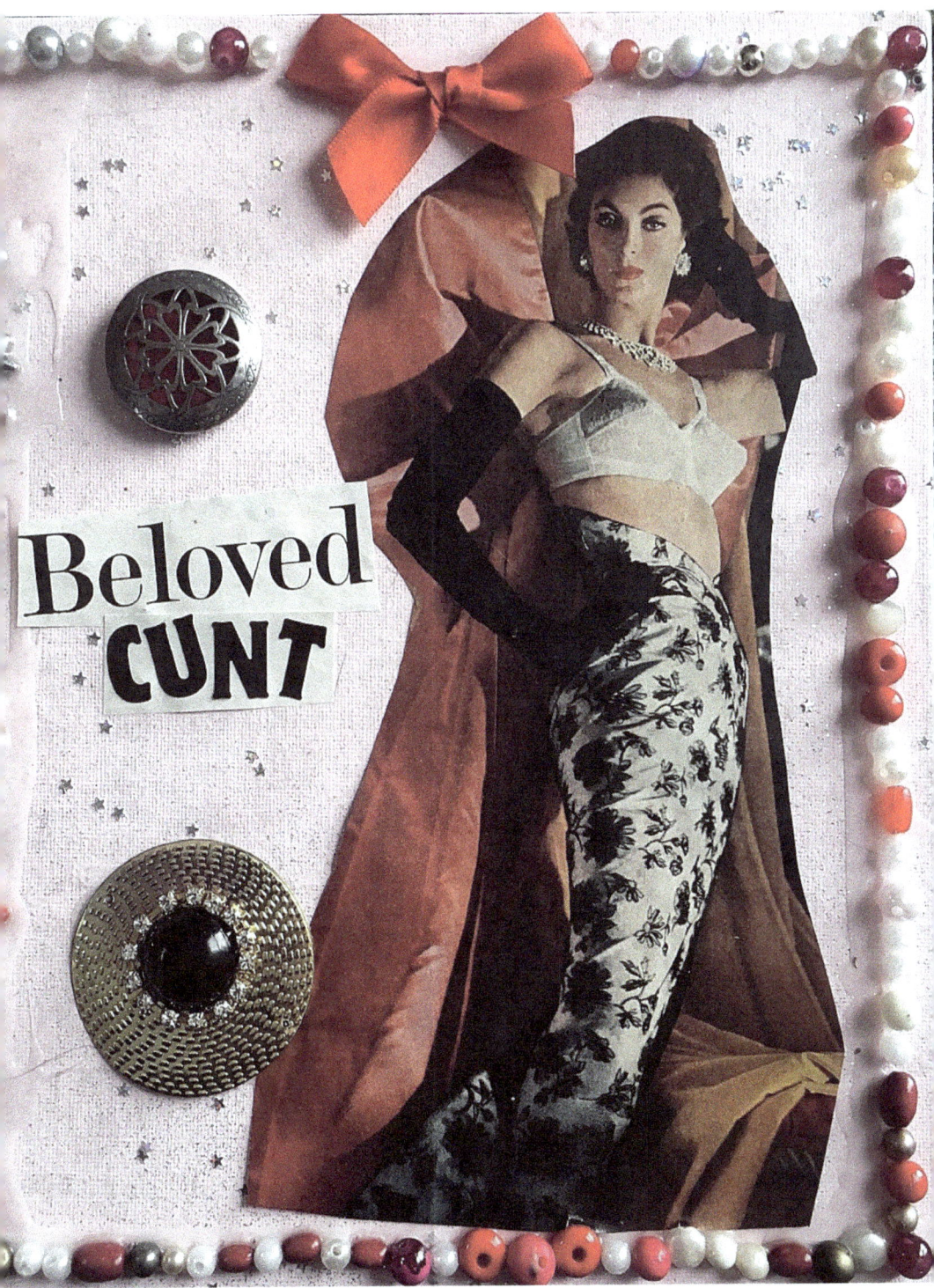

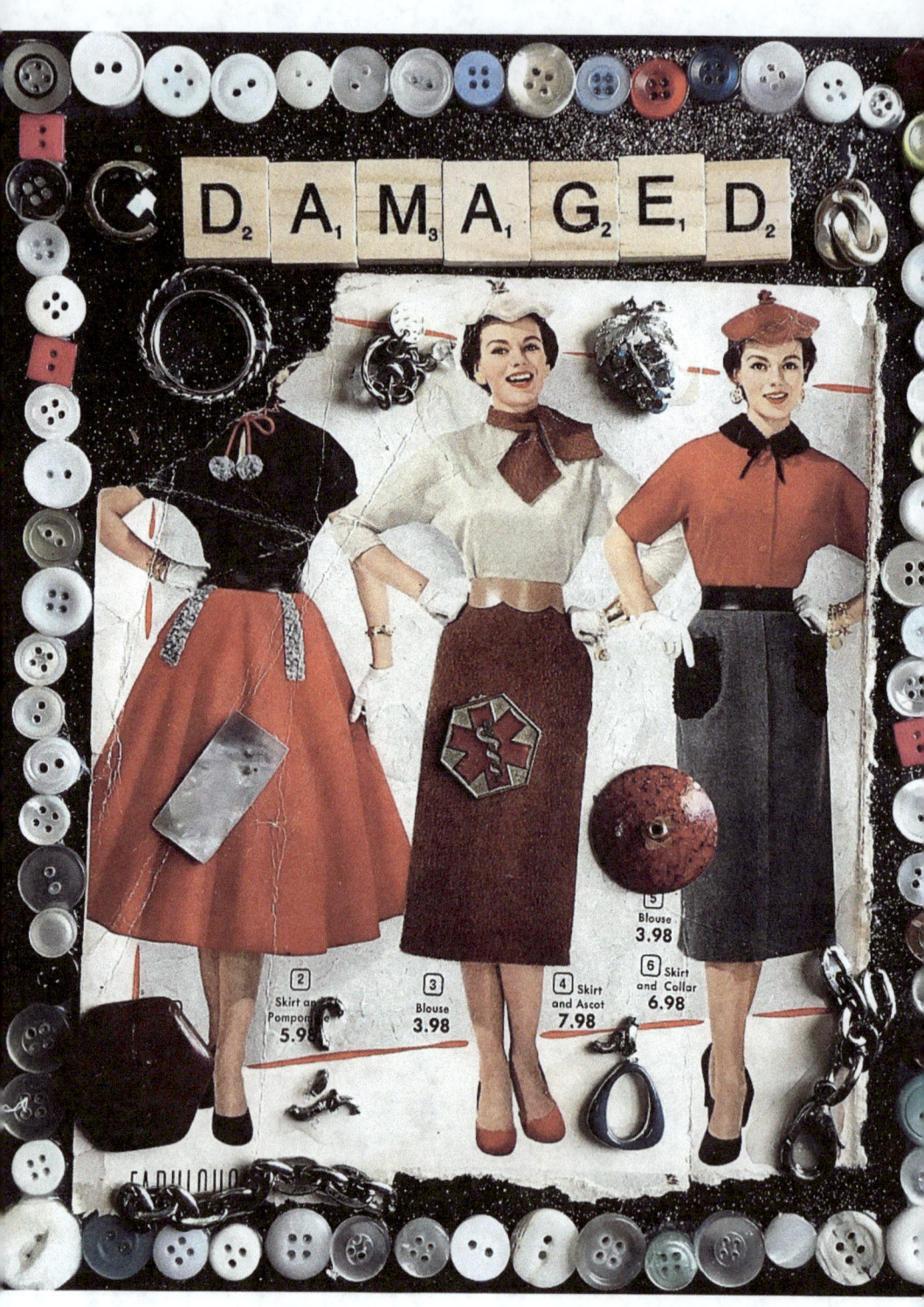

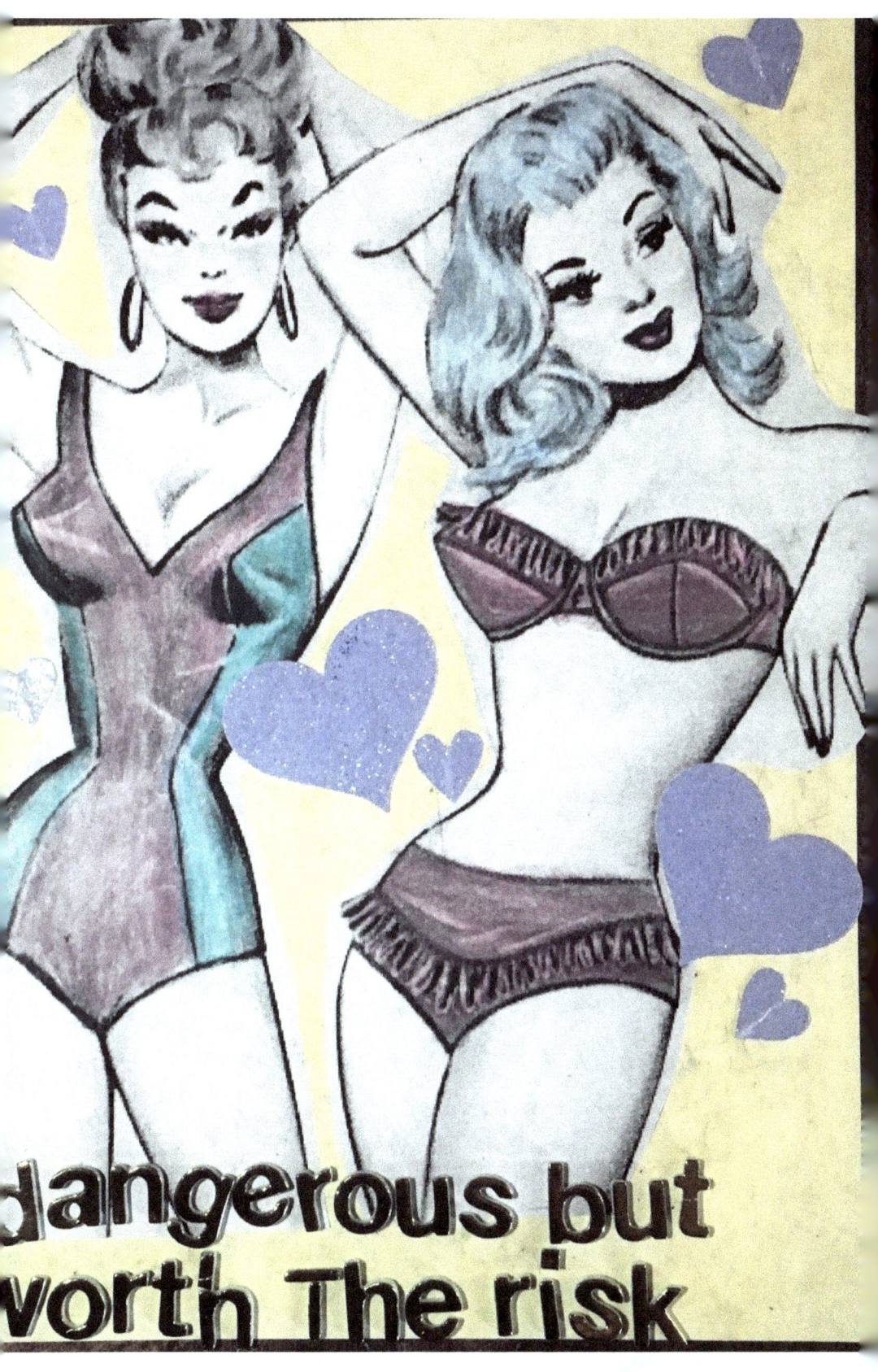

dangerous but
worth The risk

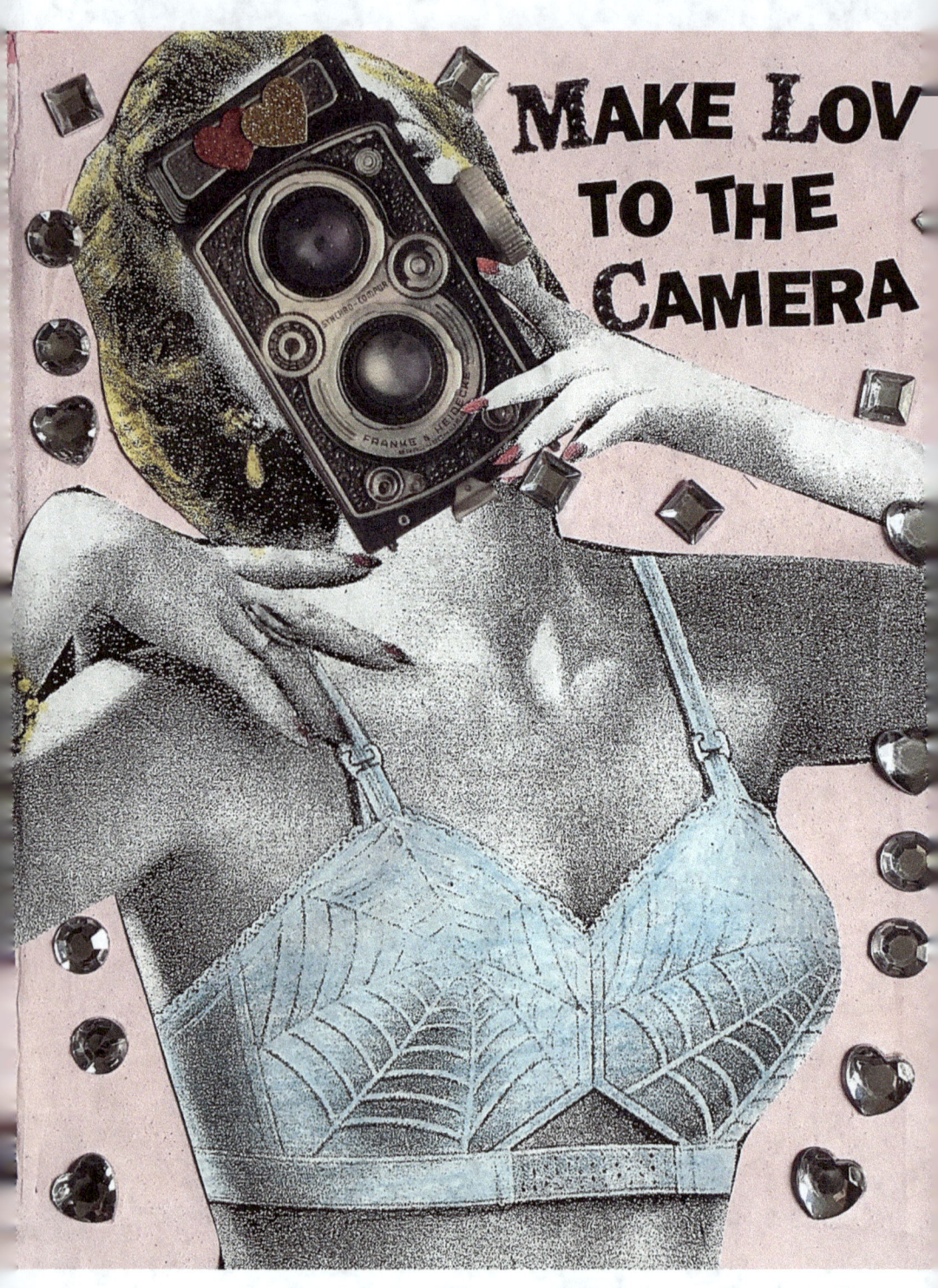

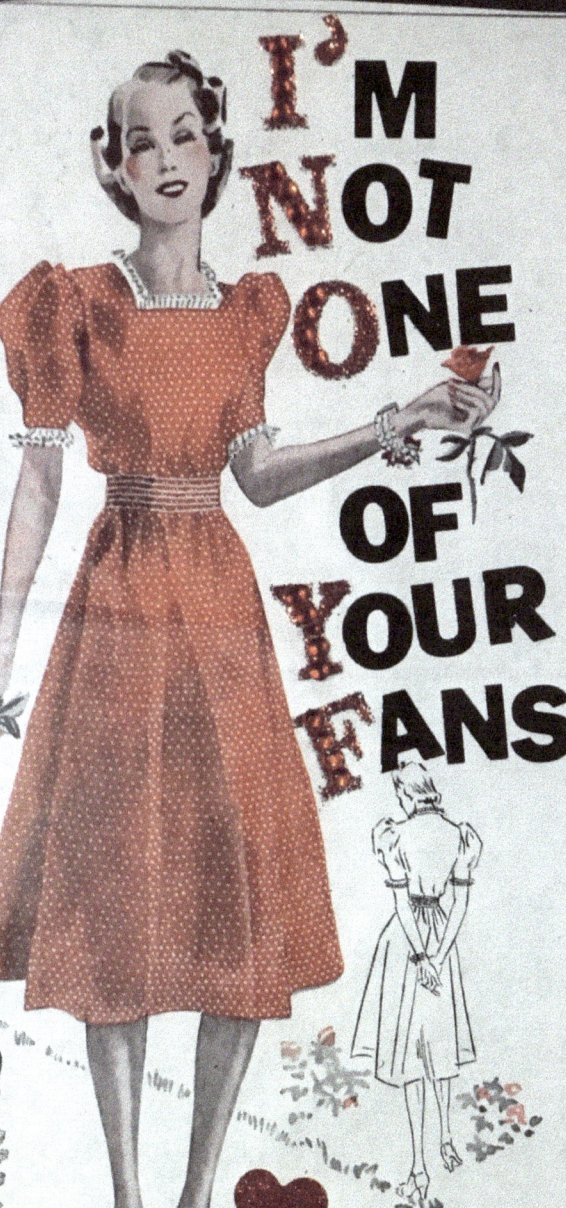

I'M NOT ONE OF YOUR FANS

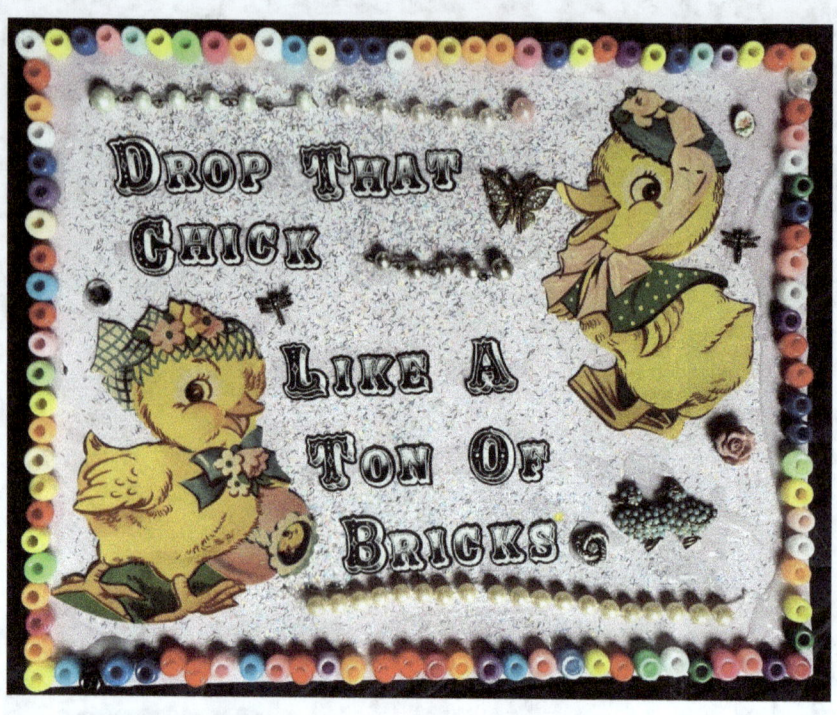

DROP THAT CHICK LIKE A TON OF BRICKS

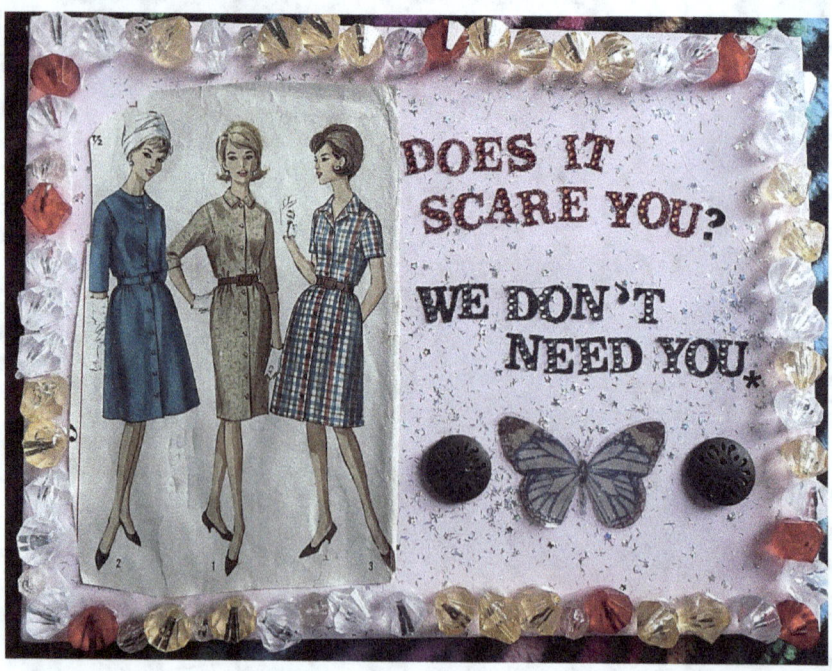

DOES IT SCARE YOU? WE DON'T NEED YOU.*

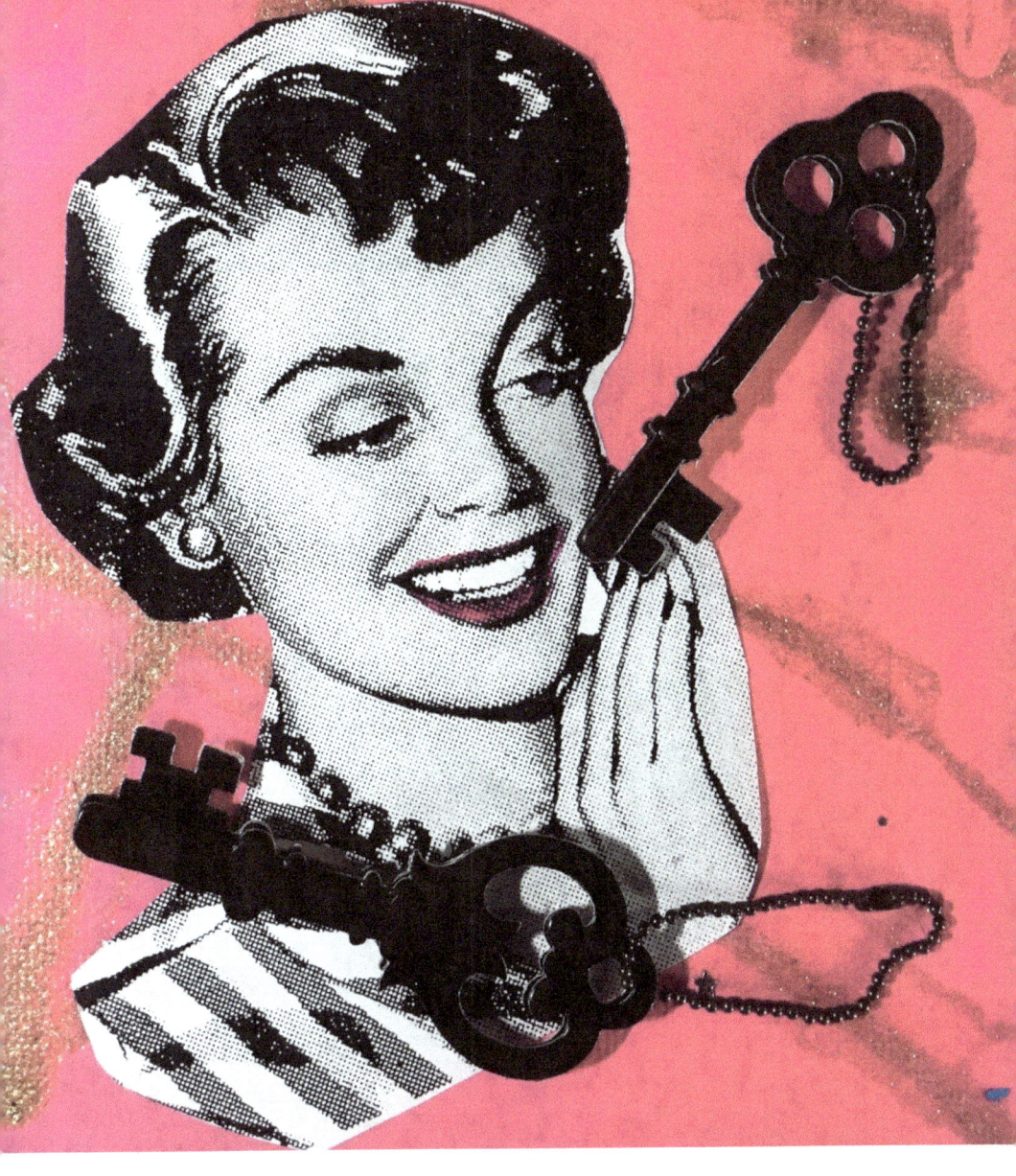

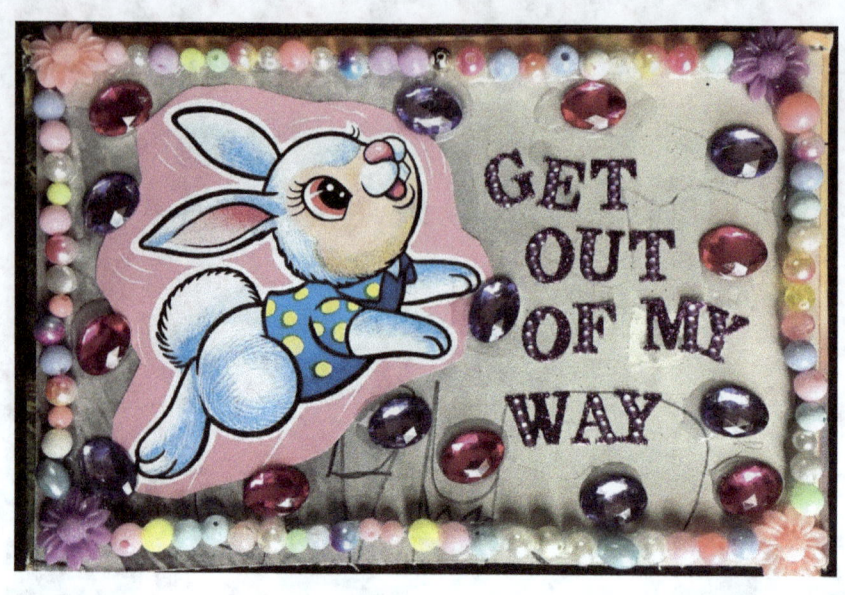

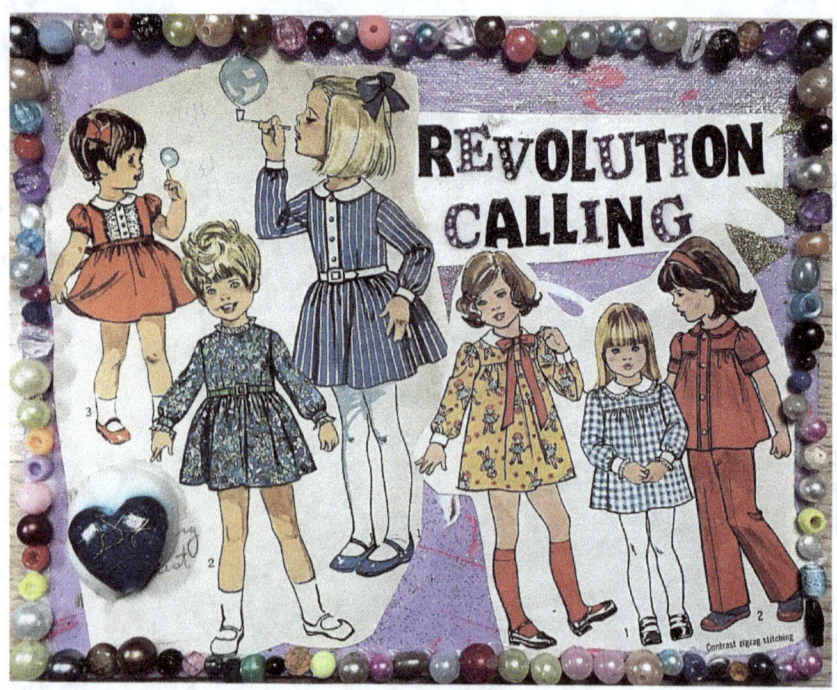

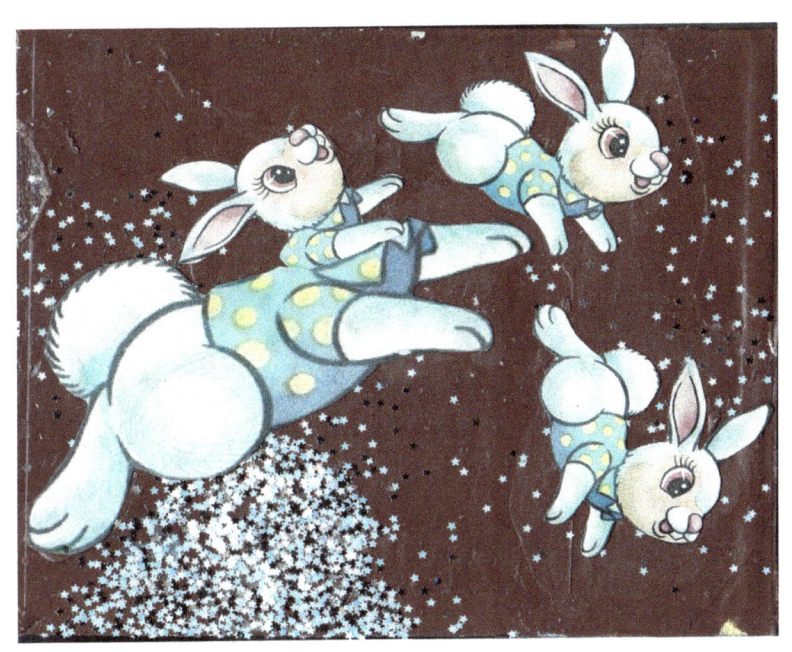

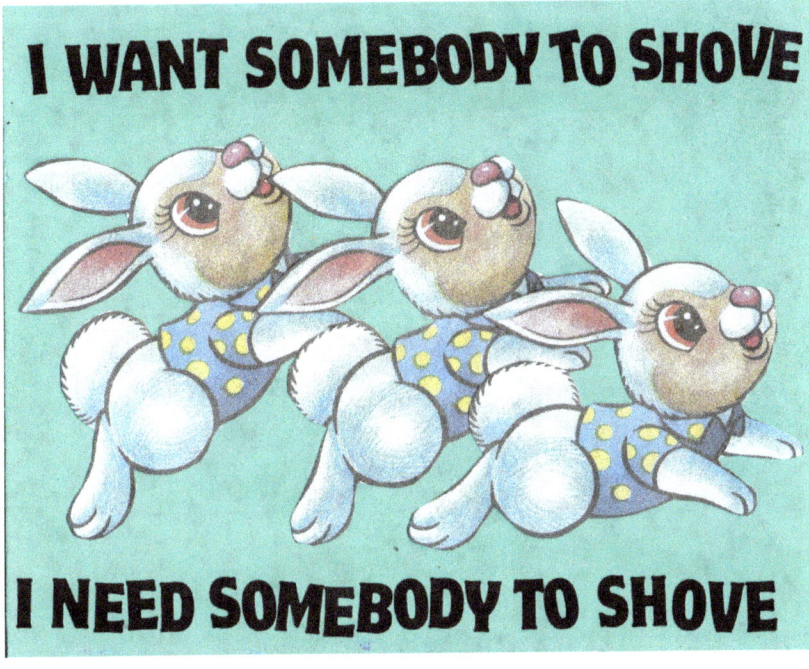

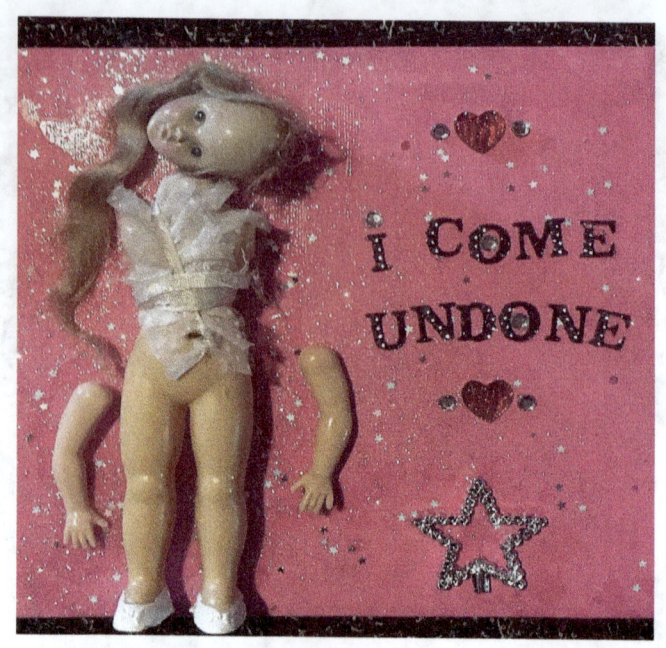

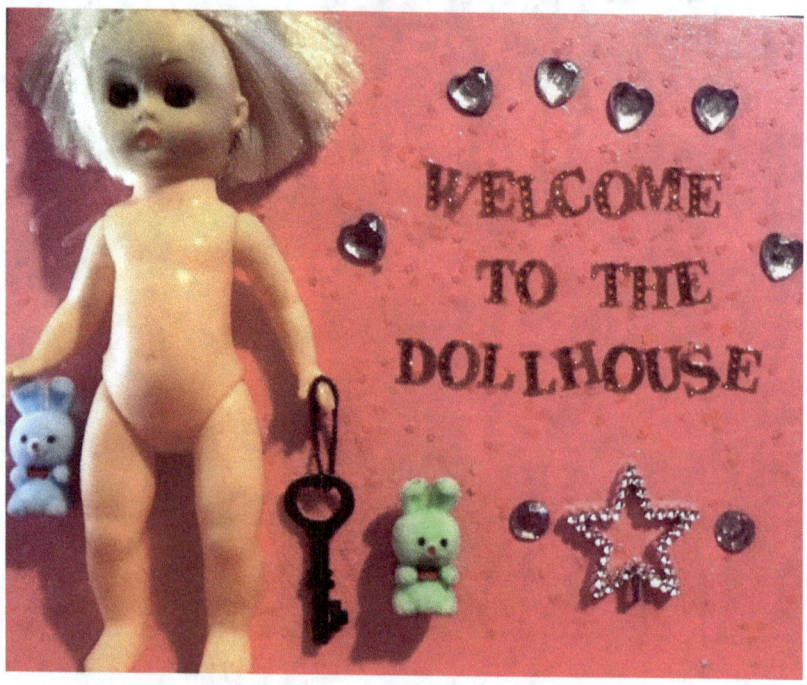

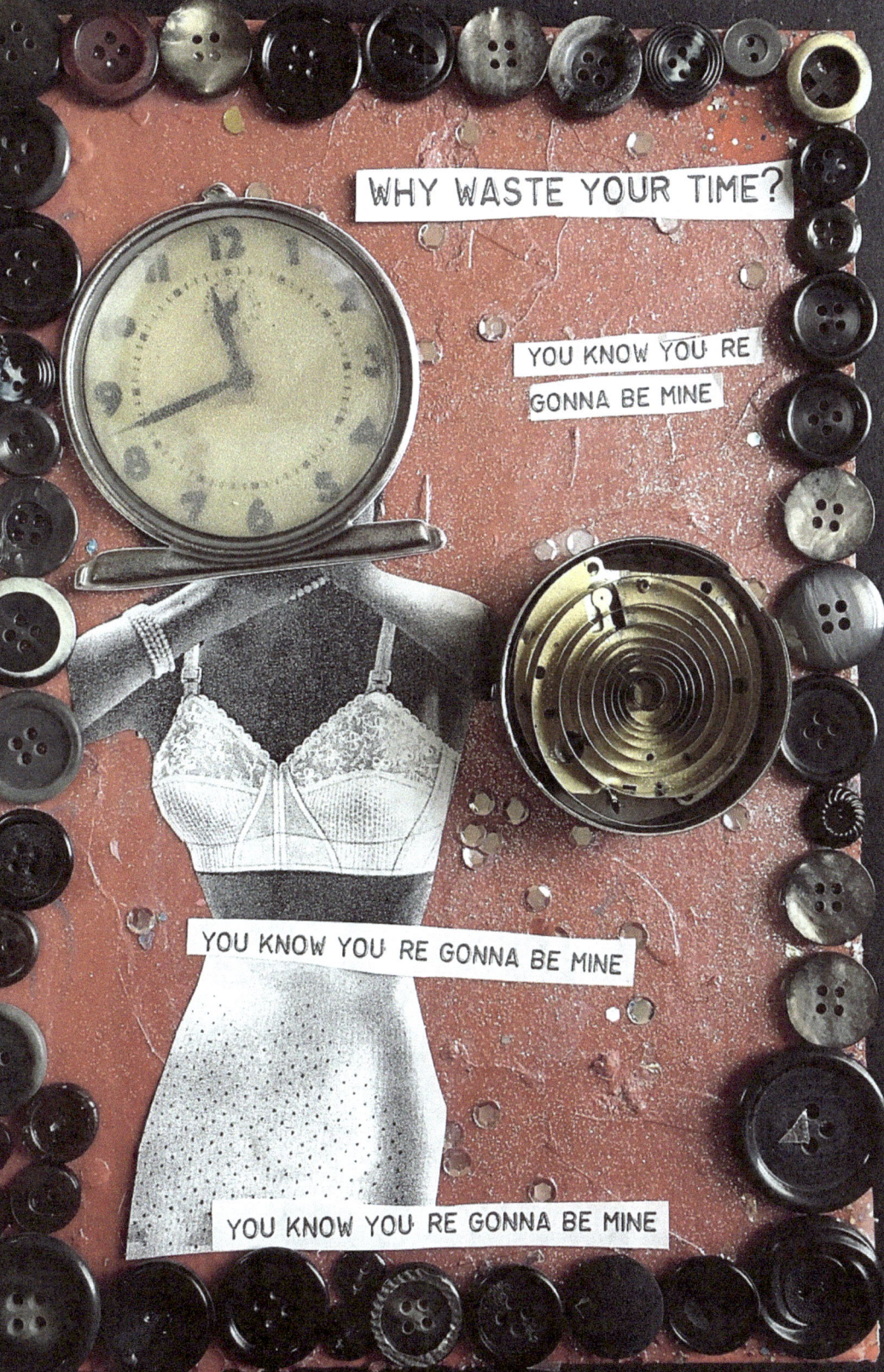

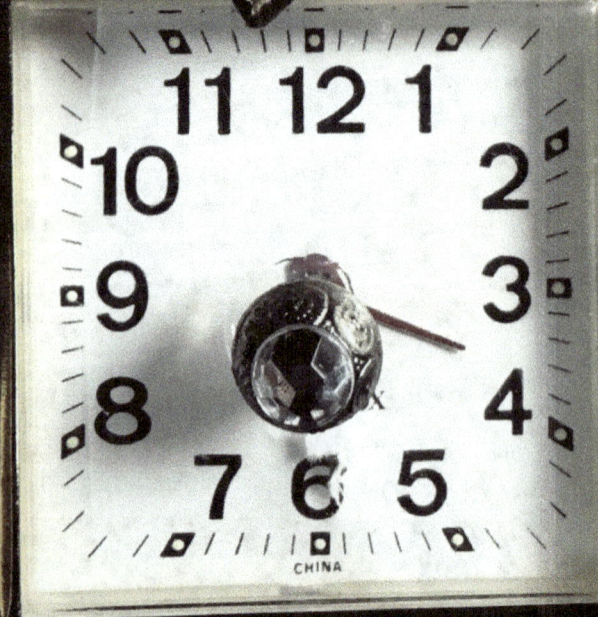

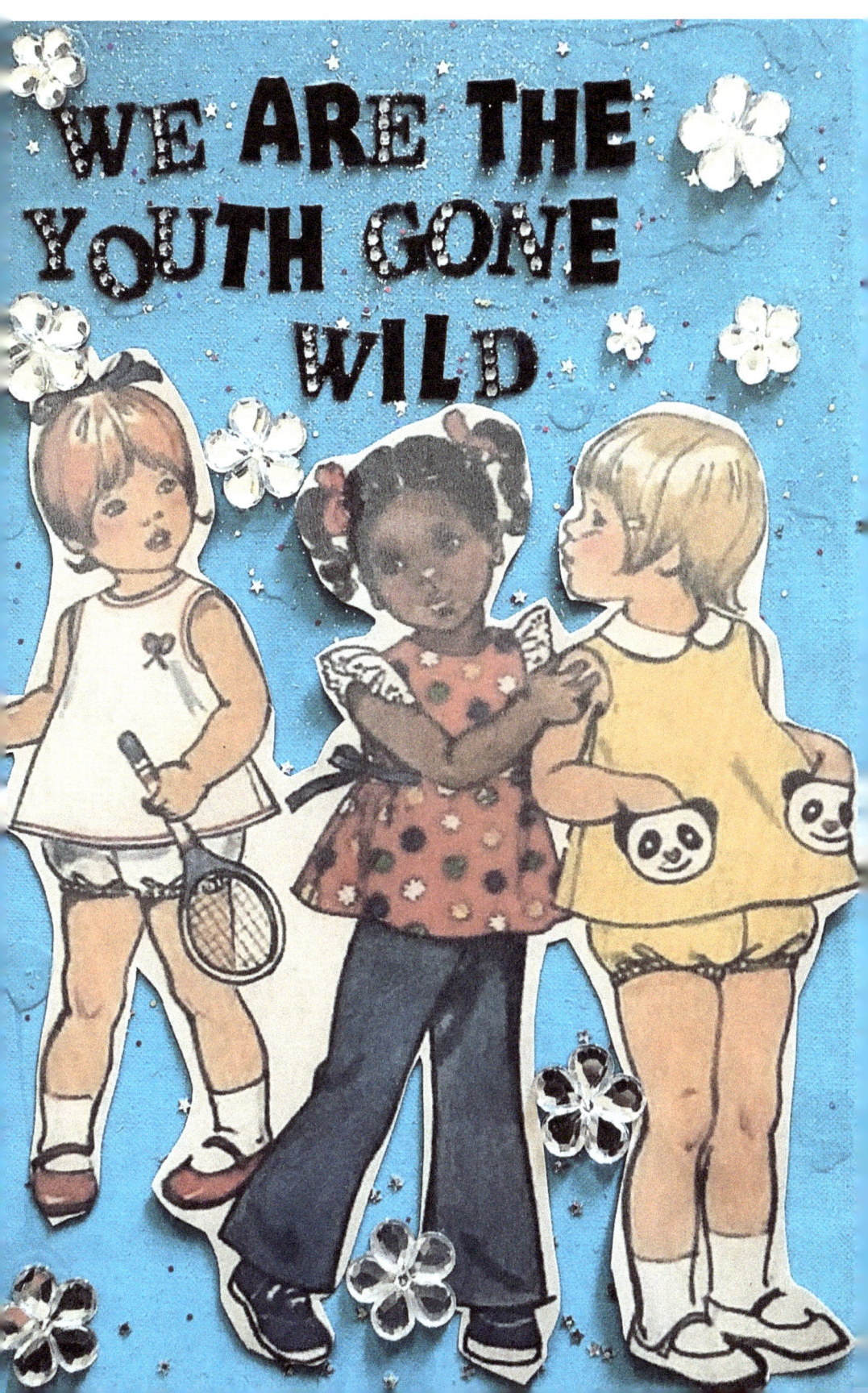

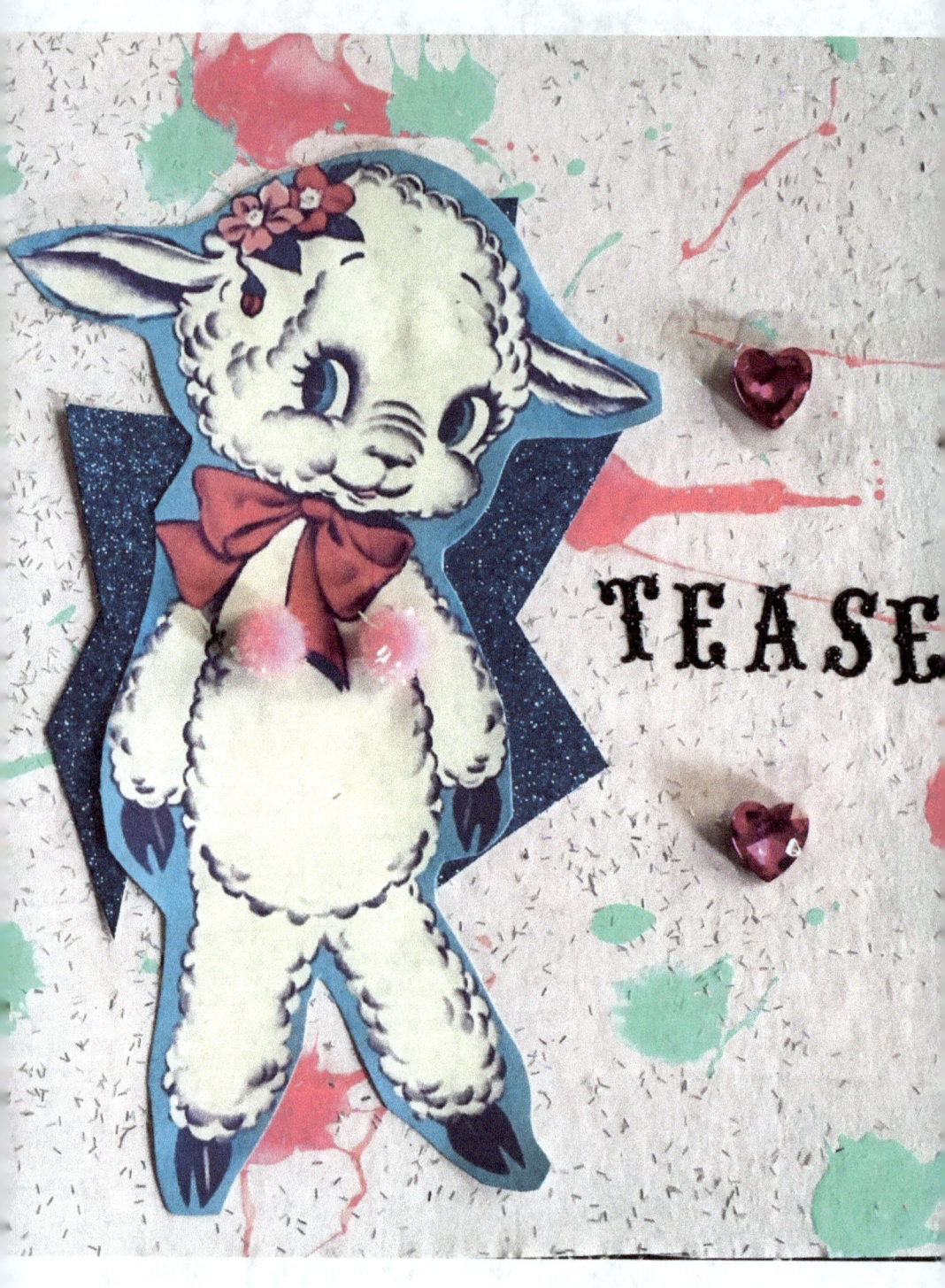

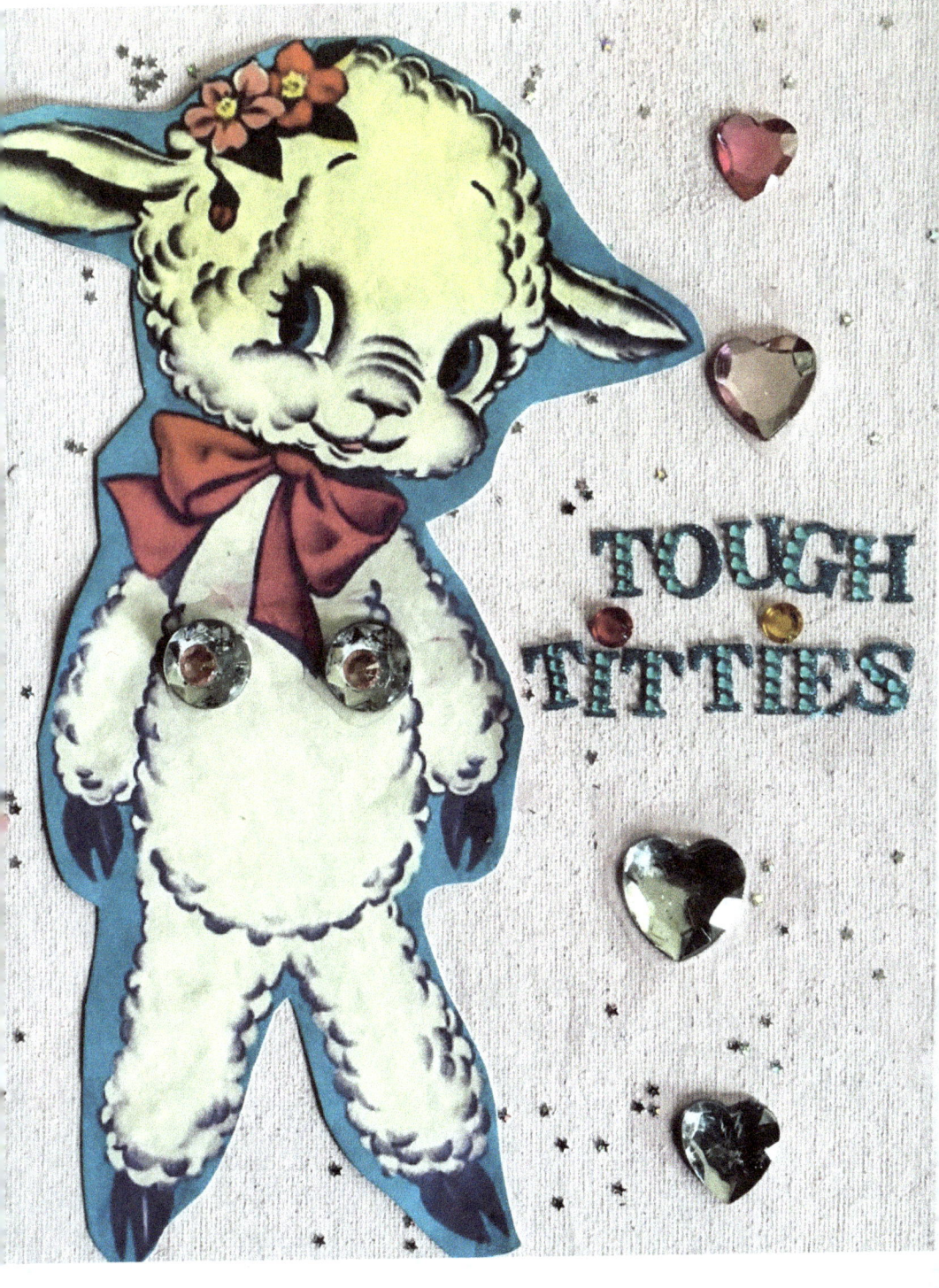

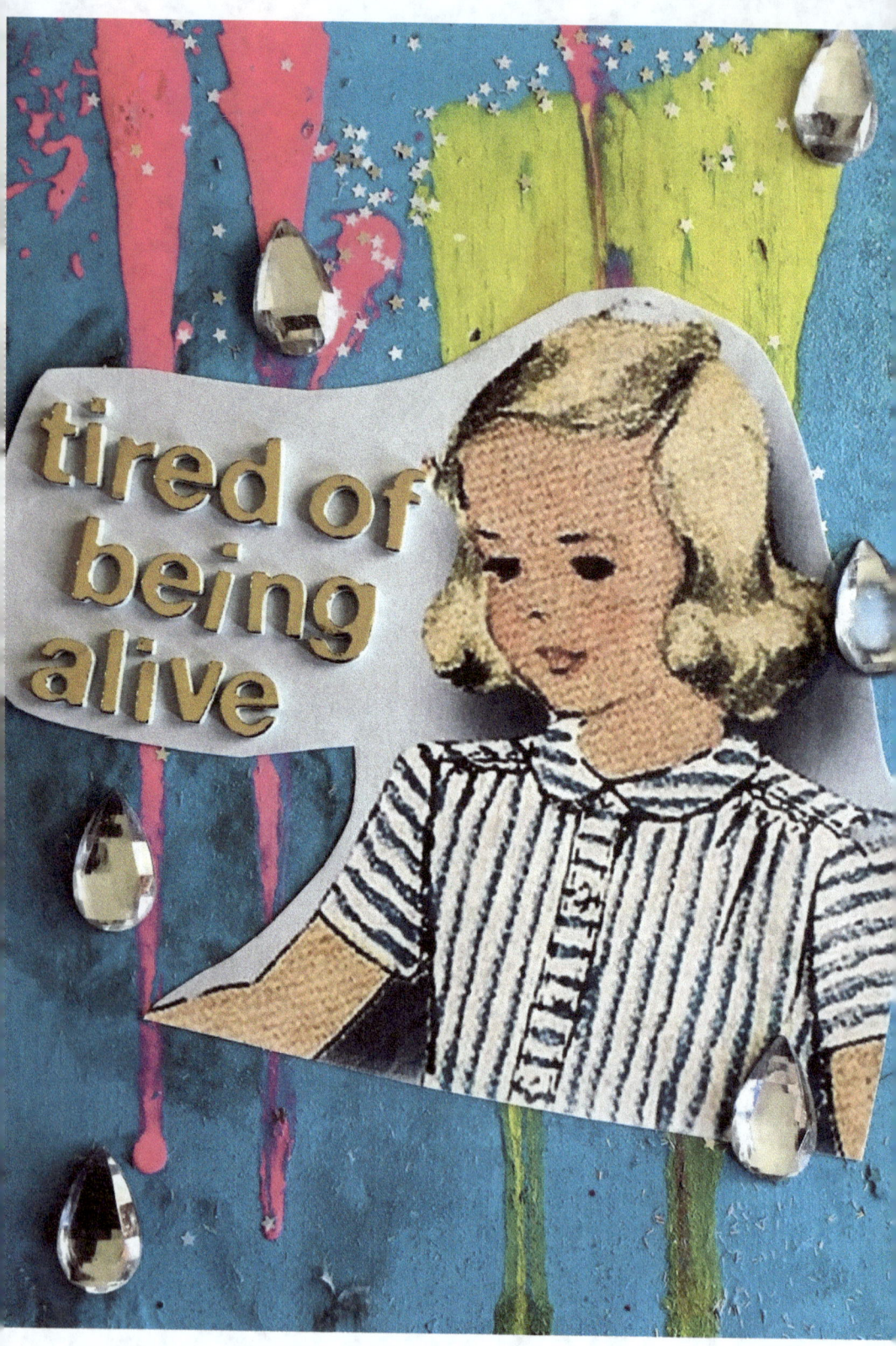

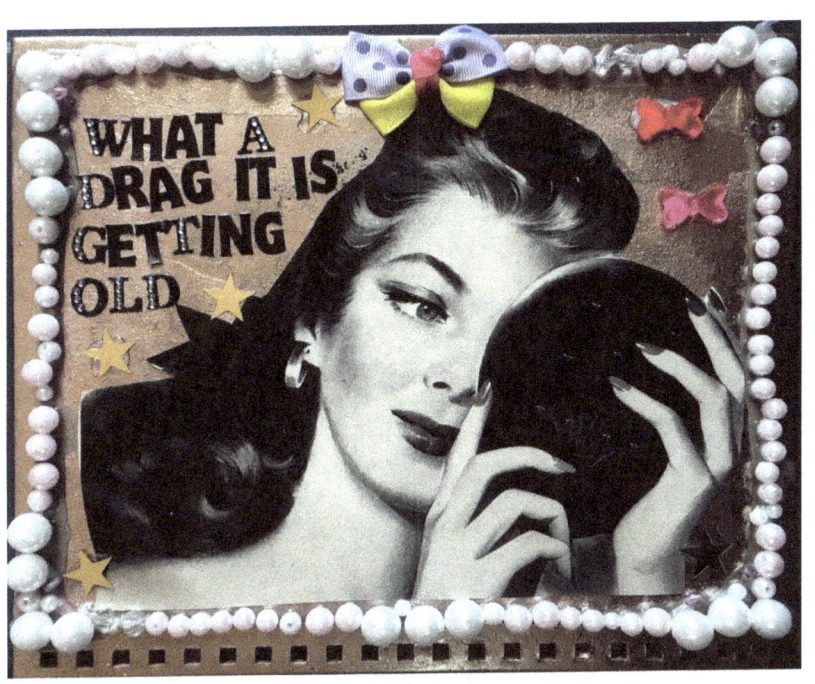

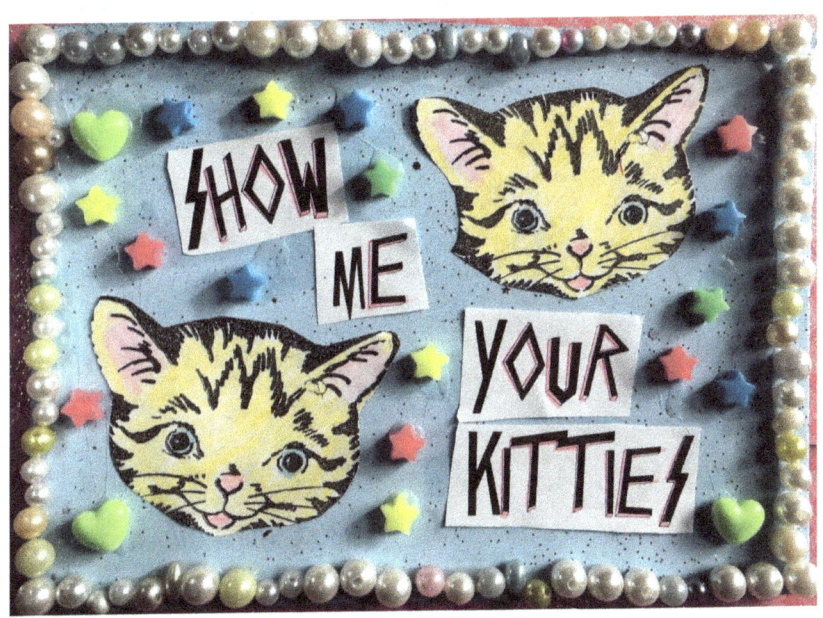

I HATE HER LIKE POISON

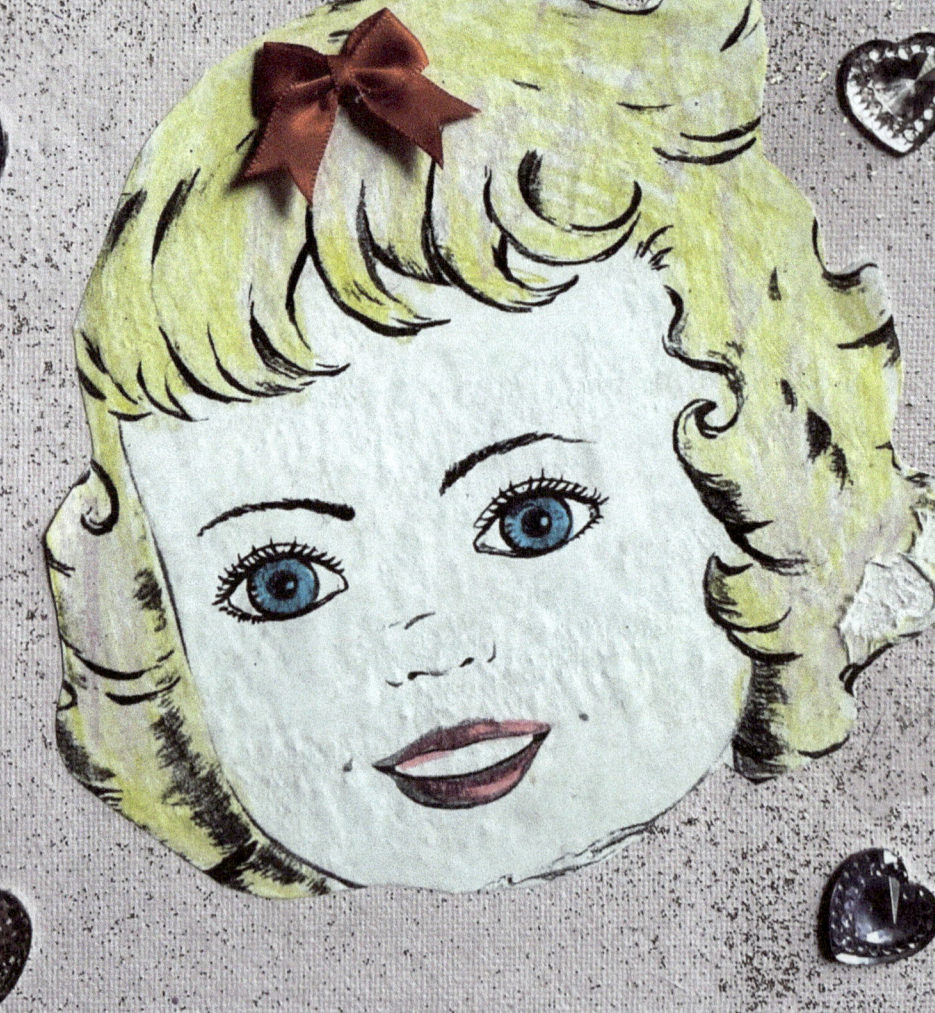

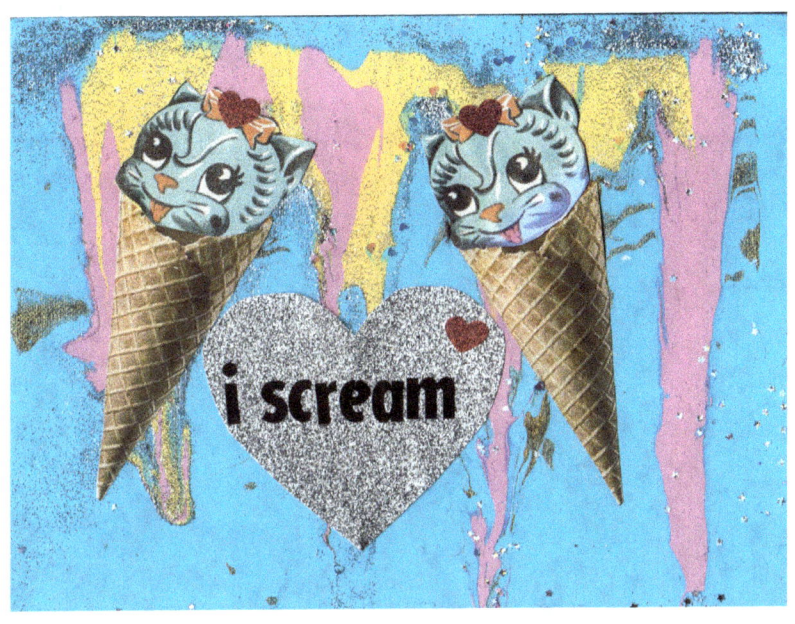

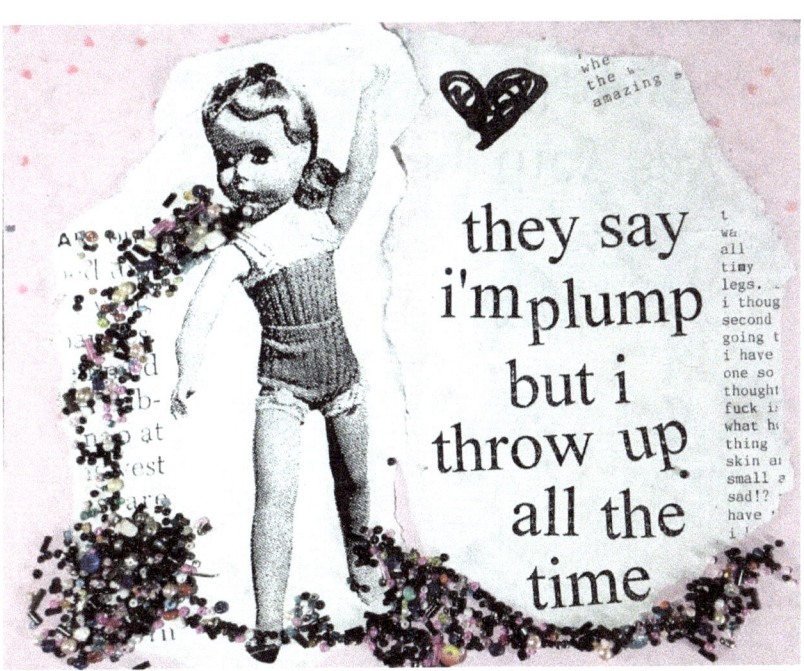

ALL GIRLS TO THE FRONT

Transfer for applique included

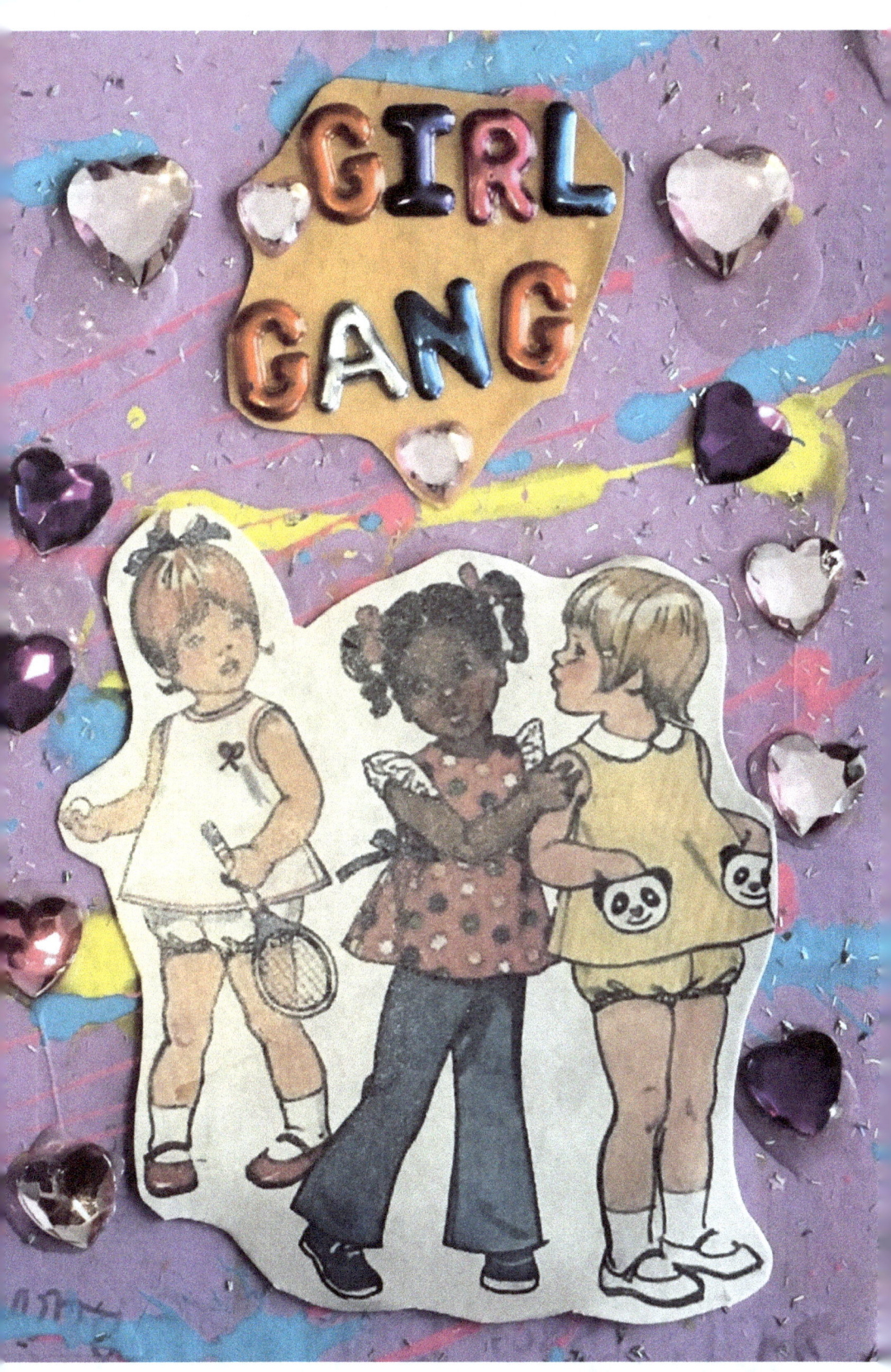

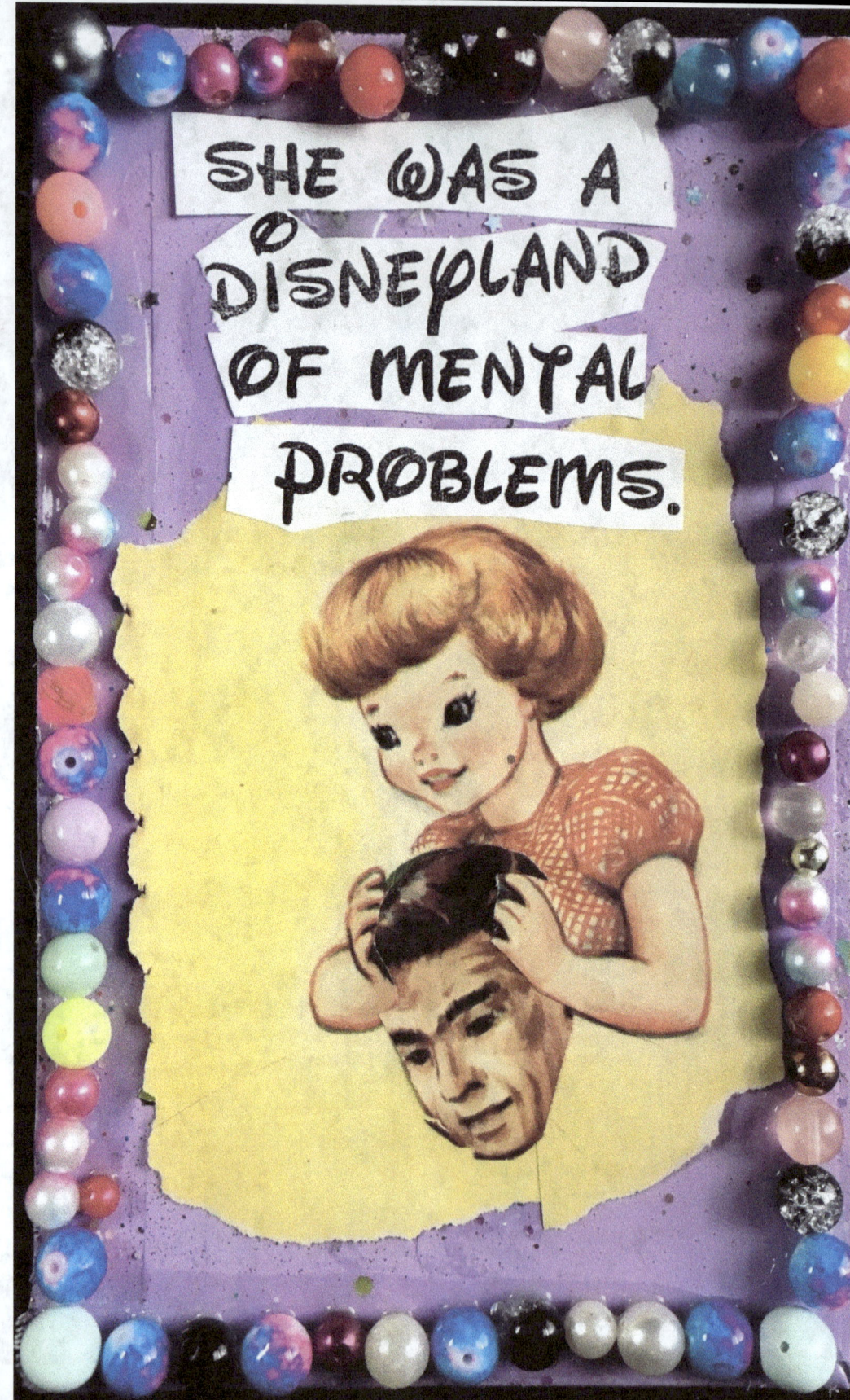

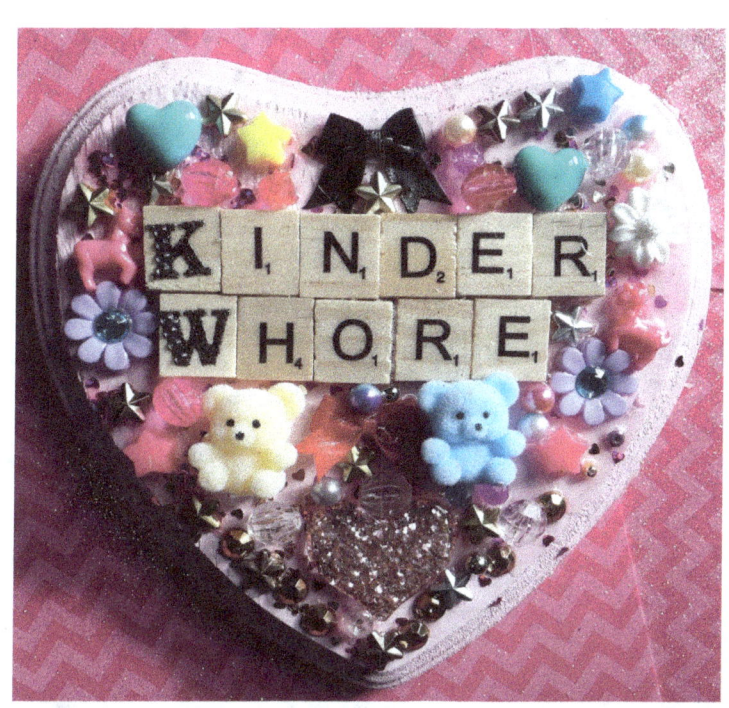

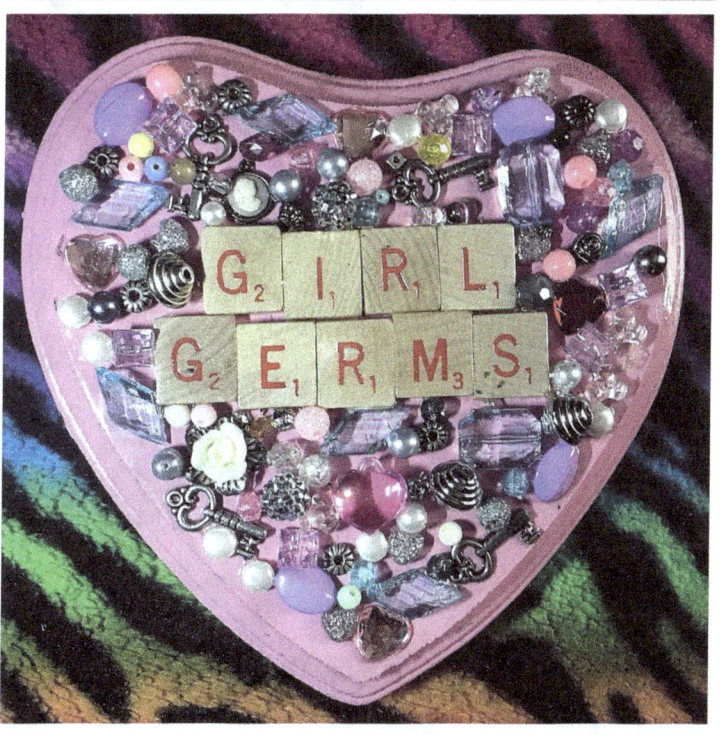

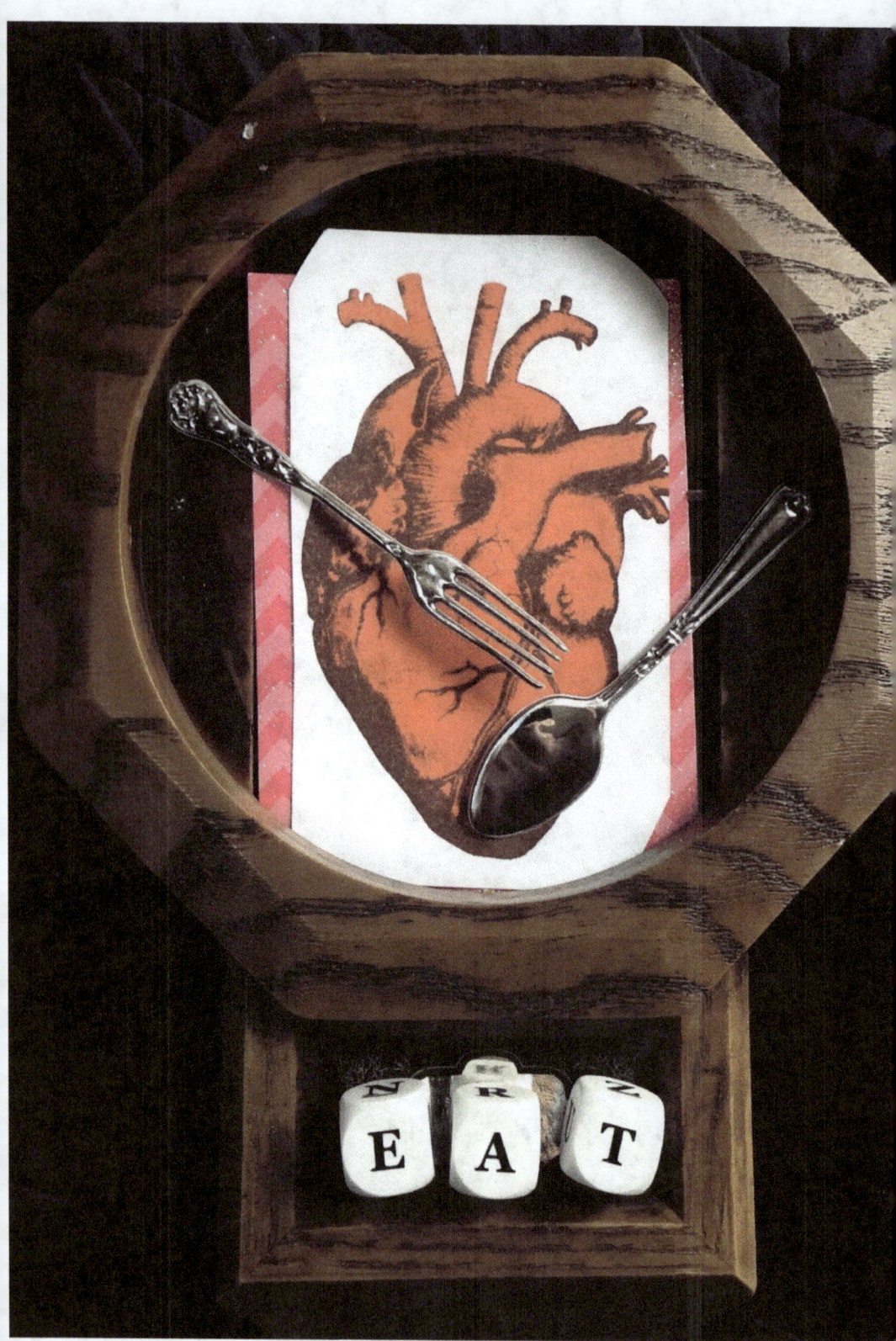

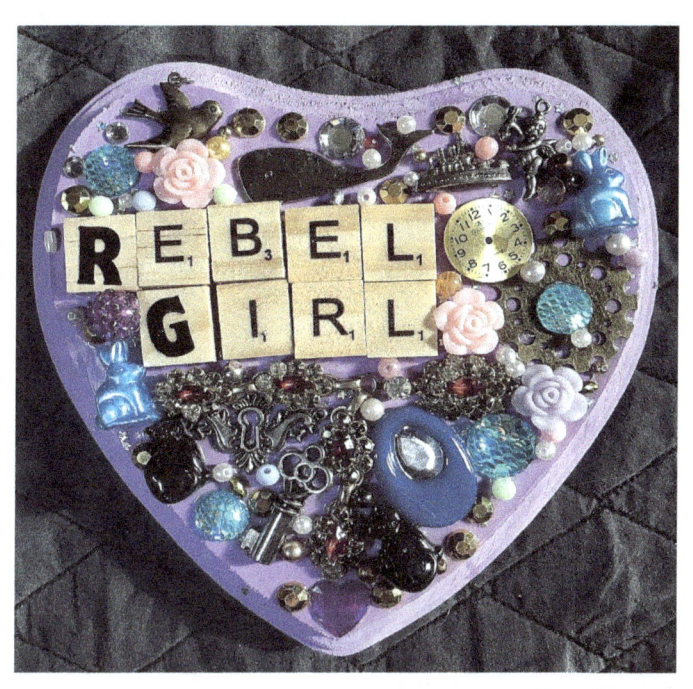

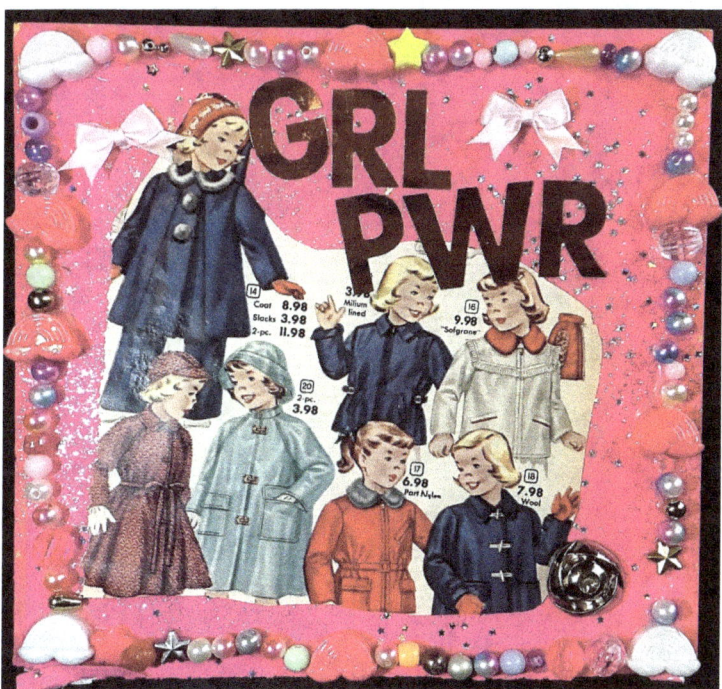

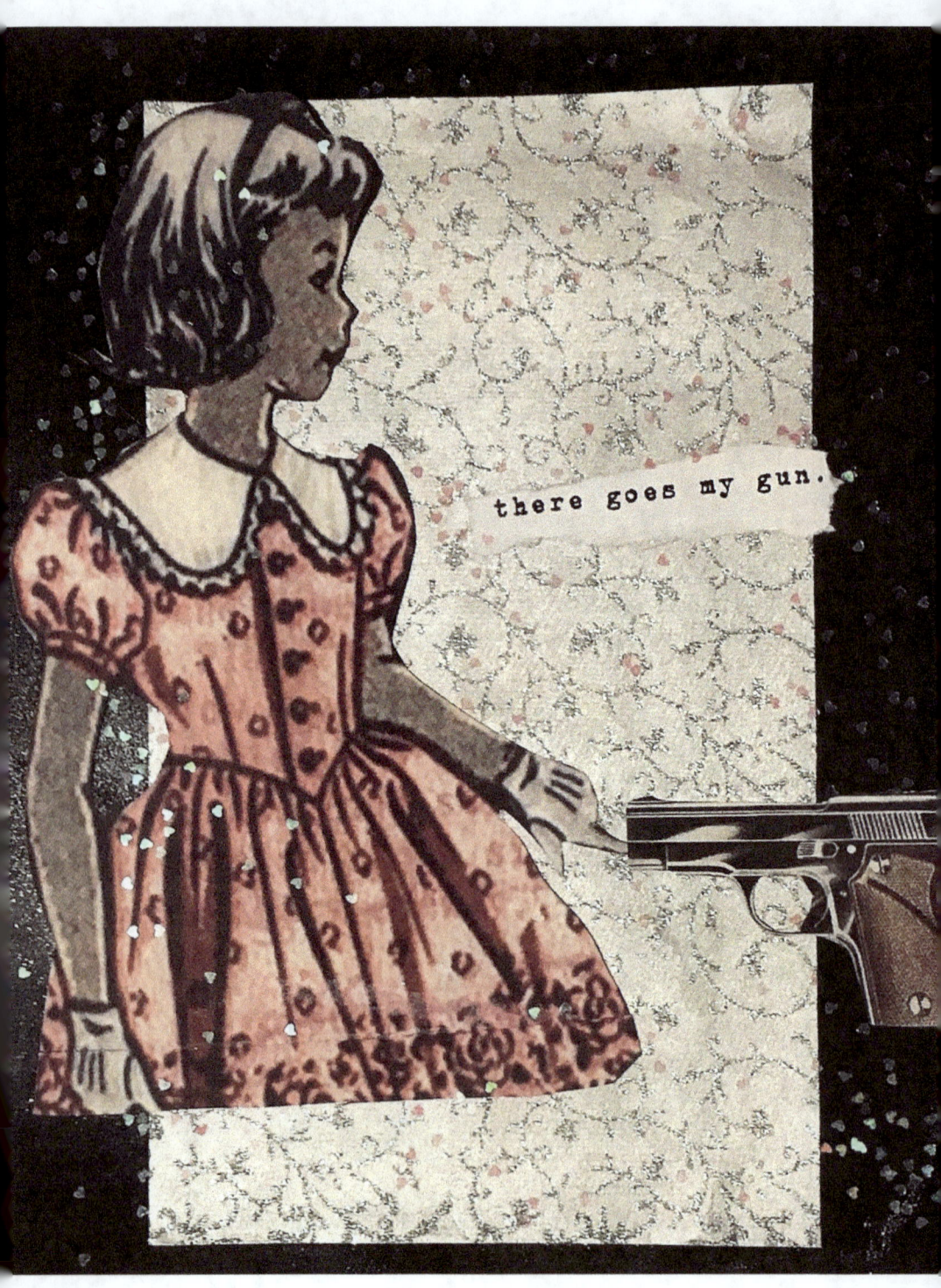

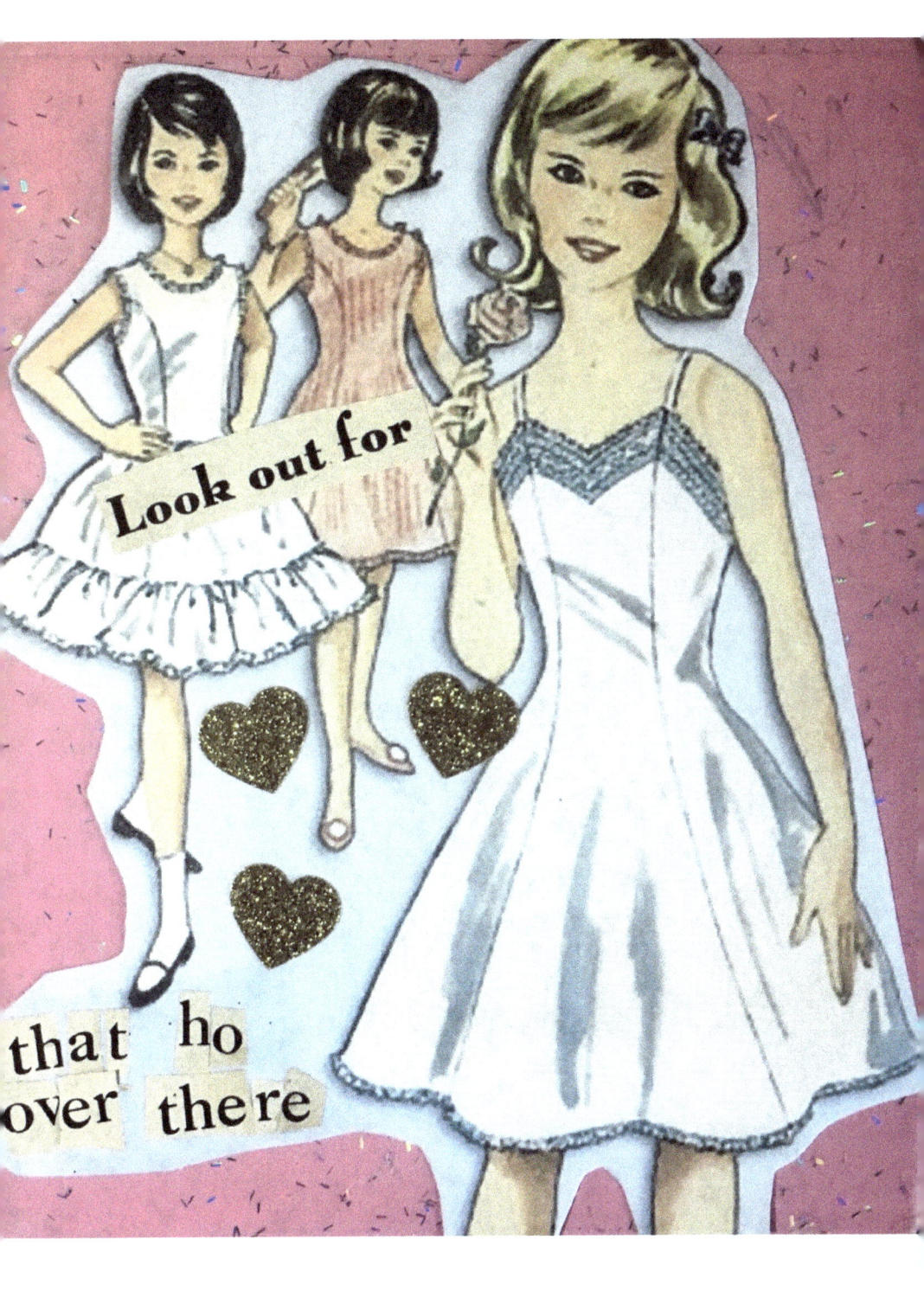

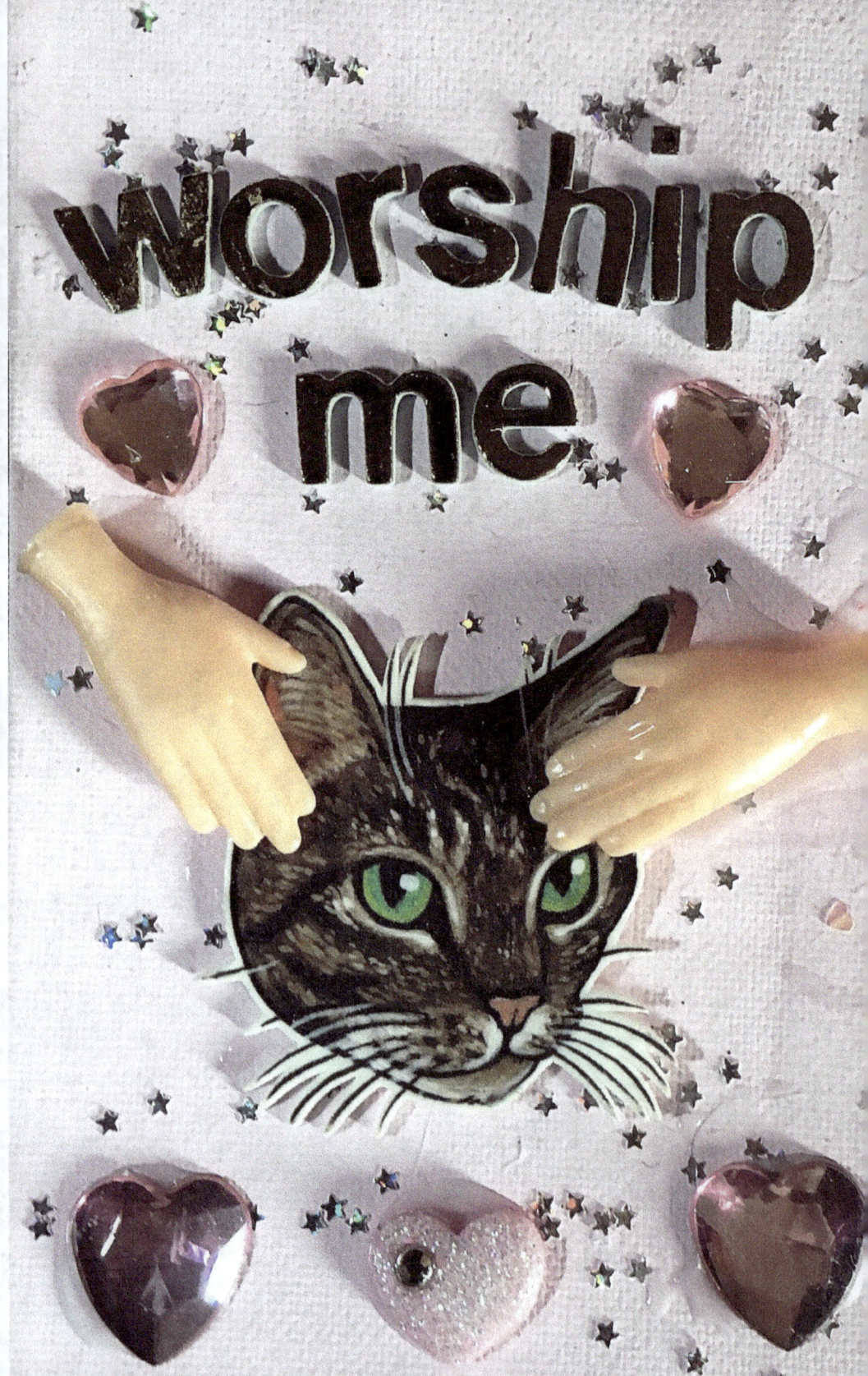

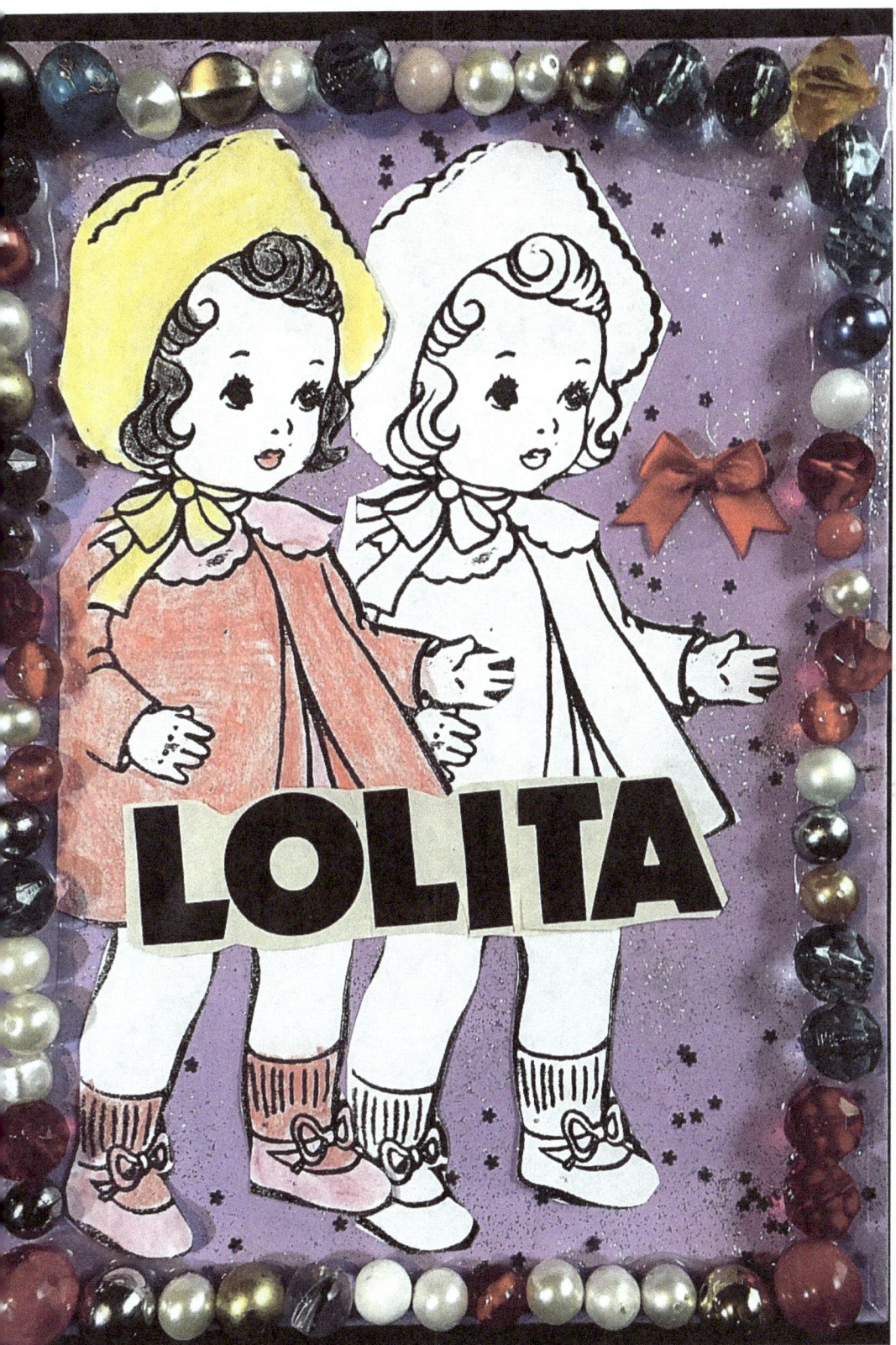

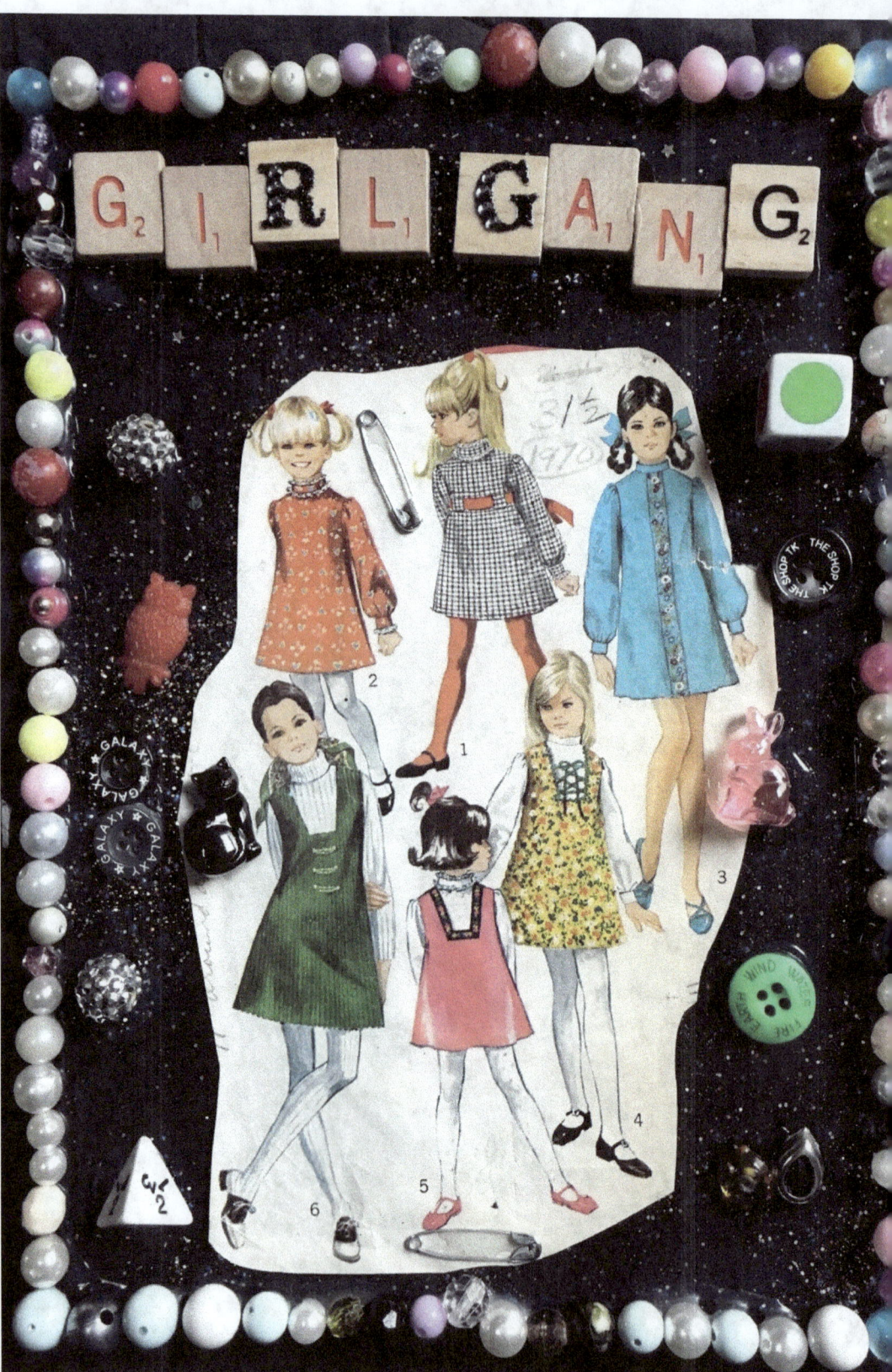

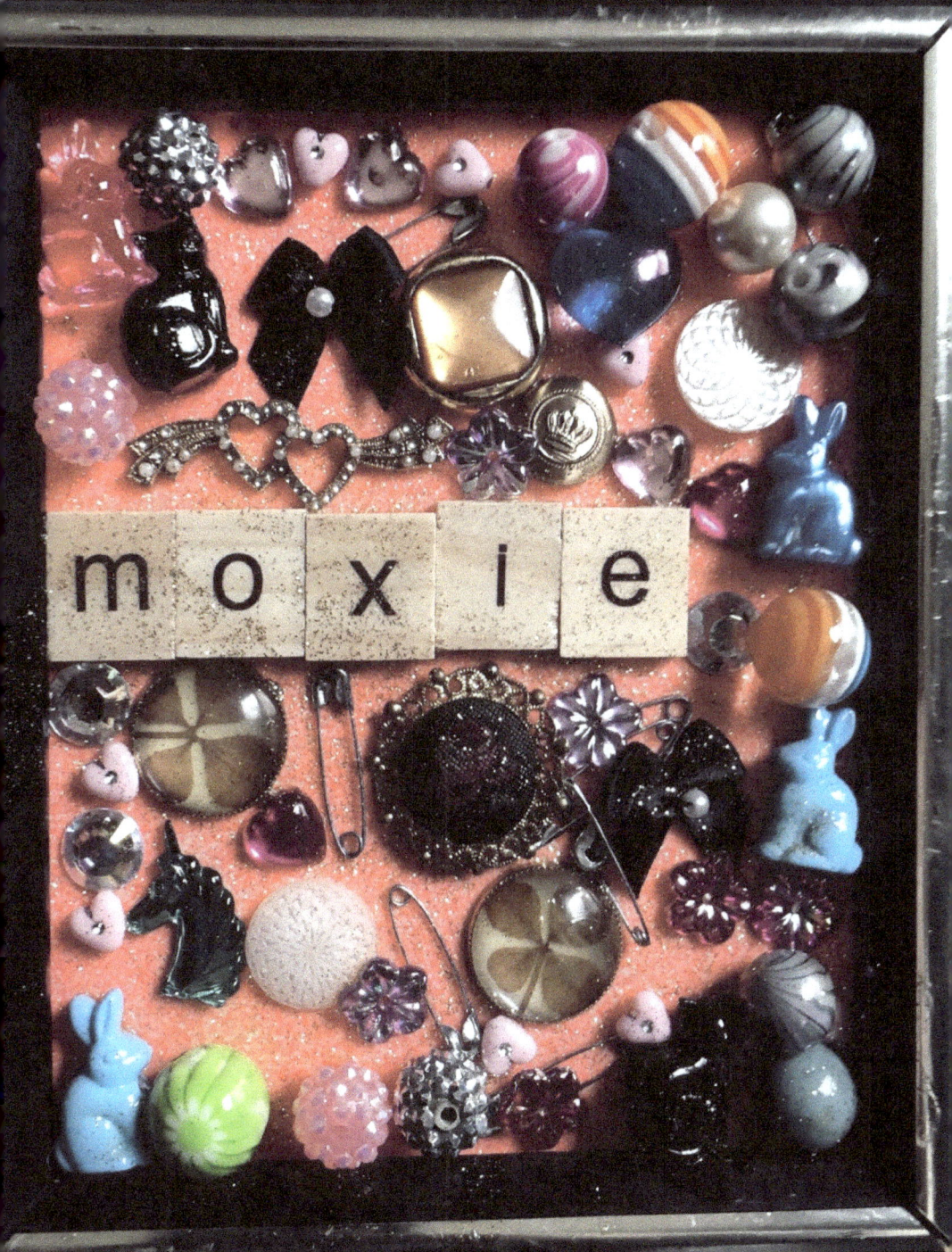

www.ingramcontent.com/pod-product-compliance
Lightning Source LLC
Chambersburg PA
CBHW070407220526
45467CB00001B/496